2004 POET

GW00600733

ONCE
A RHYME

IMAGINATION FOR
A NEW GENERATION

Southern England Vol II
Edited by Annabel Cook

Effie Pearson (11)	23
Emma Bosher (11)	24
Laura Slater (11)	25
Gemma Piper (10)	25
Ellie Bradshaw (10)	26
Nicola Gries (11)	27
Charlotte Pascoe (10)	28
Alex Paddick (10)	29
William Eales (11)	30

Hildenborough CE Primary School, Tonbridge

Bradly Watson (11)	30
Chloe Knight (9)	31
Louise Whitehead (9)	32
James Fullbrook (9)	33
Megan Terry (11)	33
Lauren Patience (10)	34
Becky Broad (10)	34
Jed Welland (10)	35
Andrew McNamara (10)	35
Toby Richards (10)	36
Stephanie Ochmann (11)	36
Suzanna Richards (10)	37
Richard Tang (10)	37
Jenny Taylor (11)	38
Stephanie Mortlock (11)	38
Sam Thompson (11)	39
Rebecca Moir (10)	39
Dominic Walkling (10)	40
Emily François (10)	40
Caitlin Witcomb (10)	41
Charlie Richardson (10)	41
Kate McBride (10)	42
Pippa White (11)	42
Philippa Edwards (10)	43
Ben Wood (9)	43
Lauren Goodchild (9)	44
Lauren Humble (10)	44
Daniel Denton (9)	45
Felix O'Leary (11)	45
Amy Coles (9)	46

Jenny Hughes (9)   46
Alexandra Coles (9)   47
Marc Hawkins (10)   47
Edward Clark (10)   48
Ross Johnson (10)   48
Eleanor Raishbrook (10)   49
Adam Newton (9)   49
Sophie Worsfold (10)   50
Lydia Regis (10)   51
Flo Simpson (9)   52
Jessica Lipington (10)   53
James Plimmer (9)   54
Tom Iliopoulos (10)   55
Molly Noble (9)   55
James Tribe (10)   56
Laura Tolhurst (9)   57
Liam Kemp (9)   57
Rebecca Hird (10)   58
Oliver Kendall (9)   59
Divia Marwaha (9)   60

Hilltop First School, Windsor

Michael Corsini (8)   60
Liam Ainsby (9)   60
Hina Jaffri (9)   61
Andrea Ljungberg (8)   61
Charlotte Harmes (9)   61
Alex French (9)   62
Lucy Greely (9)   62
Callum Barrett (8)   62
Kerry Newman (9)   63
Kerry Hogg (8)   63
Cerise-Kumal Uppal (9)   63
Hamzah Riaz (9)   64
Martin Barnett (8)   64
Nathan Stevenson (8)   64
Stephanie Brench (9)   65
Max Kinsler (9)   65
Ian Bell (8)   65
Zoe King (9)   66
Charlotte Kellet (9)   66

Oaklands Junior School, Crowthorne

Alex Burrell (10)	66
Sarah Robey (10)	67
Emma Kennedy (10)	68
Ella Freeman (10)	68
Madeleine Burrell (7)	69
Natalie Thompson (8)	69
Stephanie Lovell-Read (9)	70
Caitlin O'Neill (10)	70
Jessica Lehmani (10)	71
Bethany Allen (10)	72
David Lehmani (10)	72
Kate Wood (9)	73
Daniel Bean (11)	73
Sam London (11)	74
Sophie Stafford (10)	75
Georgia Loft (8)	75
Charlotte Wain (8)	76
Robert Tolcher (10)	76
Matthew Freeman (7)	77
William Thompson (11)	77
Jess Turner (10)	78
Georgina Ross (11)	79
Imogen Murray (7)	79
Olivia Cox (10)	80
Sarah Andrews (8)	80
Lisa Field (8)	81
Lee Hopwood (10)	81
Chloe Bentley (9)	82
Gemma Field (10)	82
Rhiannon Hitt (11)	83
Charlotte Wells (8)	83
Elliott Markham (11)	84
Peter Hitt (9)	84

Parkway Primary School, Earith

Laura Coppen (8)	85
Kaliegh Jackson (9)	85
Anthony Esiape-Pinnock (9)	86
Shelly Lang (9)	86
Charlie Benn (10)	87

Peter Homewood (10)	87
Lee Bulling (10)	88
Jahvade Francis (9)	88
Victoria England (9)	89
Georgie Benton (9)	89
Kirstie Gavin (10)	90
Charlee Smith (10)	90
Rochelle Dussard (11)	90
Ryan Bulling (10)	91
Tony Hoang (10)	92

St John's Beaumont School, Old Windsor

Kris Boulter (10)	92
Alexander Alderman (10)	93
Henry Taylor (10)	93
Jeremy Ousey (9)	94
Oliver Stirling Harkin (10)	94
Chatowa Kaluba (10)	95
Patrick Vickery (10)	95
Edward Zatka-Haas (10)	96
Ben Hollins (9)	96
Shiva Chauhan (10)	97
Jason Higgins (9)	97
Benjamin Fernando (10)	98
Christopher Heywood (9)	98

St Katherine's CP School, Snodland

Stephanie Brooks (10)	99
Jessica Randall (9)	99
Charlotte Punyer (10)	100
Rebecca Merry (10)	100
George Cooke (10)	101
Natalie Bush (10)	101
Charlotte Phillips (9)	102
Alice White (9)	102
Megan Payne (9)	103
Ashley Randall (9)	103
Charlotte Huston (9)	104
Lindsey Gwilliam (10)	104
Laura Turner (9)	105
Lauren Baker (10)	105

Rachel Andrews (9)	106
Sam Shaw (9)	106
Sam Robinson (10)	107
Ryan Williams (9)	107
Kirsty Brooker (9)	108
Jessica Archer (10)	108
Georgia Smith (10)	109
Samantha Berry (10)	109
Declan McMorrow (10)	110
Charlotte Bungay (9)	110
Declan O'Connell (10)	111
Geoffrey Robinson (10)	111
Natasha Manning (9)	112
Rose-Jane King (9)	113
Chloe Johnstone (11)	114
Sophie Ellis (9)	114
Christopher Carr (10)	115
Laura Roope (11)	115
Jordan Penney (10)	116
Ryan Fuller (9)	116
Matthew Punyer (11)	117
Samantha Stevens (9)	117
Tom Jarmyn (10)	118
Matthew Cradduck (11)	118
Ethan Martin (11)	119
Rebecca Field (11)	119
Nicola Paget (10)	120
Keith Jenner (10)	120
Chloe Manning (11)	121
Daniel Crosby (9)	122
Aisling Gilham (11)	122
Reece Allen (10)	123
Catharine Laverty (11)	123
Aaron Baxter (10)	124
Michael Stevens (10)	124
Katie Filmer (7)	124
Lauren Ivy (7)	125
Katy Morgan (10)	125
Alex Scott (11)	125
Hannah Morgan (7)	126
Ben Kember (8)	126
Leanne Tattersall (8)	127

Tanya Sterrett (11)   142
Tom Crittenden (10)   142
Sarah Kendall (11)   142

St Paul's CE Primary School, Swanley Village
Colleen Fitzpatrick (7)   143
Alex Chapman (9)   143
Thomas Franklin (7)   143
Jaymie-Leigh Horn (11)   144
Daniel Ludlam (10)   144
Dean Baldwin (10)   145
Laura Franklin (10)   145
Thomas Morey (9)   146
Oliver Coe (9)   147
Sonny Exeter (10)   147
Lucy Evans (9)   148
Gareth Clarridge (11)   148
Daniel Humm (10)   149
Chloe Webb (9)   149
Laura Townson (11)   150
Hannah Waddington (10)   151
Harry Oborne (10)   151
Alice Spinola (8)   152

St Peter's CE Combined School, Slough
Jamie Buggy (8)   152
Charley Ringer (8)   153
Maverick Davies (8)   153
Jovi Wilson (9)   154
Rumbi Mukundu (9)   154
Jamie Byne (9)   155
Jonathan Pomry (9)   155
Cameron Lovett (9)   155
Victoria Garnett (8)   156
Crystal Yang (9) & Jesskiran Kullar (8)   156
Lindsey Tanner   157
Kerri Thomas (9)   157

St Teresa's Catholic Primary School, Wokingham

Harry McGill (7)	158
Alice Graham (7)	158
Megan Marks (7)	159
Imogen Stone (8)	159
Lucy Farrell (7)	159
Anna Jones (8)	160
Megan Shillibier (7)	160
Elliot Ball (8)	161
Paige Blake (8)	161
Joel Grist (8)	161
Amy James (7)	162
Gemma Boucher (7)	162
Catherine Barnes (9)	162
Antiana Loxha (8)	163
Thomas Mitchell (9)	163
Jack Murray (8)	164
Joseph Crolla (8)	164
Gabby Pitts (8)	164
Jack Hughes (9)	165
Sophie Hastings (8)	165
Eloise Utley (8)	166
Alicia Clark (9)	166
Alice Wilson (8)	167
Lauren Olivia Booth (8)	167
Hannah Lyle (8)	167
Bethan Davies (8)	168
Hannah Poland (8)	168
Sasha Gama (8)	169
Sarah Rafferty (9)	169
Matthew Sanderson (8)	170
Nicola Relf (8)	170
Judith Taylor (9)	171
Aaron Morjaria (9)	172
Matthew Dodington (8)	172
Meg Martin (9)	173
Olivia Reilly (8)	173

Seabrook CE Controlled Primary School, Hythe

Kirstie McFarlane (8)	174
Jason Jordaan (8)	175

The Poems

Match Of The Century

The match we've all been waiting for.
Everyone expects Ronaldo to score.

Finally we see our favourite teams, Man U and Madrid
The crowd never cheered like they just did.

During the match Giggs kicked Zidane hard.
Fouls like that deserve the yellow card.

Figo took the free kick, the ball soared.
Ronaldo kicked it in, the crowd roared.

The kick-off was taken by Phil and Gary Neville
It was up to Ruud to make it level.

They thought he would score they even bet,
He did, he put it in the back of the net.

To Madrid kick off was taken by Figo and Zidane.
To the ball strikers Ronaldo and Raul ran.

Finally Ronaldo ran and got it.
Off the pitch, though, the ball was hit.

The corner was taken by O'Shea
The ball curved and went the wrong way.

It went to Raul he kicked it in.
Manchester's hopes were in the bin,

Scholes scored; it went to extra time, the players ran
The penalty shootout was fine for each Madrid fan.

They all scored; it went to another set
Ronaldo hit the ball in the back of the net.

Ruud tried to answer his team's call.
But Sanilas dived and blocked the ball.

The match had ended, it was done.
The champions league, Madrid had just won.

They took the team photo and sprayed the champagne
It was the beginning of Madrid's European reign.

Barath Nair (10)
Buxlow Preparatory School, Wembley

The Fourth R-Riot

Susan and Sally,
Were the reason the riot began,
Susan punched Sally,
Who immediately choked on her ham.
David at once started singing.
Then decided to do it twice,
So Mary started teasing,
Our very own class mice.
Then the teacher walked in and everyone went quiet,
She said 'Now stop this, stop this raging riot!'
All we had to do was bow our sorry heads,
As nothing more was left to be said,
Unfortunately we had detention for weeks after that,
Luckily it was not our jobs,
Otherwise Susan and Sally would have been sacked!

Hannah Breen (10)
Buxlow Preparatory School, Wembley

My Mind Is Blank

Desperation!
I don't know what to write
As I can't think
The paper is still white.
My mind is blank not knowing what to do.
But here I am,
Scribbling something
I wonder if I'll ever be able to think.
I have these scary creatures running around my head
I look deep inside my mind sometimes and
I feel like I don't know a single thing.
But then it comes
Inspiration!

Daniyal Gohar (10)
Buxlow Preparatory School, Wembley

If I Had A Pet

If I had a pet I would play with it all day long.
If I had a pet I would always sing it a song.
If I had a pet I would cuddle it all night long.
If I had a pet I would feed it when I heard the birds' song.

If I had a pet I would keep it out of danger.
If I had a pet I would keep it away from any stranger.
If I had a pet I would put it in a manger.
If I had a pet I would protect it like a ranger.

If I had a pet my face would be filled with glee.
If I had a pet I would not have to plea.
If I had a pet my mother would see,
How well I would take care of it.
If only I had a pet.

Keshini Patel (10)
Buxlow Preparatory School, Wembley

The Haunted House

I was walking from the park one day,
And there I saw *It*
It was a tall haunted house.
Thunder and lightning struck
You could not hear anything,
Not even a squeak of a mouse or even a duck.

I heard a little creak from the door.
I stopped! Now I heard *It*
I stepped closer to the door
I pushed hard and saw webs.
The floorboards squeaked,
I was to go further.
So I ran far, far away.
I don't know where *It* was
Even today.

Dajanee Lindo-Lewis (10)
Buxlow Preparatory School, Wembley

Maths

My teacher has brown hair,
Which she carries around everywhere.

It is all curly,
Probably because she is a girly whirly.

She has a scarf which is frilly,
If I put it on me it would look silly.

My teacher is so kind,
She will always be in my mind.

My teacher is the best,
So whenever I think about her I cannot take a rest.

I went to teach in a school,
Where all the children are cool.

I want to teach arithmetic,
Which will not make the children sick.

I want to be the best of teachers
I want to teach children to be good creatures.

Priya Changela (10)
Buxlow Preparatory School, Wembley

Fall!

I sat on the wall,
I had a great fall,
I bumped my head,
I fell off the bed,
I sat on the seat,
I had a great peep,
I heard a sound,
It was me on the ground.

Priya Doshi (8)
Buxlow Preparatory School, Wembley

The March Of The Dead

The march of the dead
The skeleton's plight.
The whirr of my wings.
As I take flight.

The march of the dead
My life is at stake.
The night slowly rises
As the demons awake.

The march of the dead
The strong stench of bile.
The scurry of my feet
As I tread the long mile.

The march of the dead
A pot of fresh tears.
As I creep through the tunnel
Nobody hears . . .

Olivia Majumdar (10)
Buxlow Preparatory School, Wembley

Snowy Winter

The snow falls and touches the ground
Children playing and screaming aloud,
Blazing fire, wrapped up warm.
The snow is blowing, it is a growing storm.
Snowmen with scarves
Yells mixed with childish laughs.
Grey skies with gloomy clouds
Stations filled with big crowds,
Hot chocolate in big mugs
Parents worried by the cold, giving their kids big hugs
Snowmen melting away
Children sad, waiting for another snowy day.

Sophia Kleanthous (10)
Buxlow Preparatory School, Wembley

Liverpool FC

My favourite team is Liverpool,
They are simply the best,
I wonder how much better they can become,
With Michael Owen and his pace.

The stadium that now has everything you need,
Belongs to Liverpool and their great team,
It is unlike that disastrous time,
When it was packed and people died.

The kit that the stars wear,
Is red and white with a golden glint.
When the team does win at home a famous song is sung,
'You'll never walk alone' the crowd do chant.

Some players are skilful; some are strong,
Some are good at crossing; some at scoring,
But the best I feel, who do the least of all,
Are the players in goal; the ones who stand tall.

Daniel Harrison (10)
Buxlow Preparatory School, Wembley

Seasons

Some seasons are colourful
Others are truly wonderful.
Spring is the first one
The season for having fun.
Next comes summer so merry and bright
Where no one ever has a fight.
Then comes autumn, when the leaves fall
Off the branches which are rough and tall.
Finally comes winter so lovely and white
Everyone loves it, especially at night.

Akshay Prinja (8)
Buxlow Preparatory School, Wembley

Colour

There is colour in the sky
Blue, yellow and bright
There is colour in the sunset
Brown, orange and red
There is colour in cement
Grey, blacky and lead
There is colour in a rainbow
Violet, green and indigo
There is colour on a peacock
Silver, red and yellow like my sock
There is colour on a swallow
Black, blue and a beak of yellow.

Chloé Debrah (9)
Buxlow Preparatory School, Wembley

Games Lessons

On Friday afternoon our games lessons begin
No one wants to drop the ball
But Betty almost does.
Throw the ball, catch it and throw it again
But Betty is such a pain.

Everyone thinks it is all so much fun
But Emily says she is tired.
1,2,3 throw the ball
Hope it lands in the goal.

Teacher says no one won
We did (of course).
I played a blinder
Shame about the score
But teacher says it was a draw!

Priyanka Patel (11)
Buxlow Preparatory School, Wembley

The Star

The star is a diamond,
A shining beaming one,
That constantly gleams,
Which makes our world so bright.

It glows in the pitch-black sky,
Making constellations everywhere.
I've found a dog!
So have I!
There's lots of pictures in the sky.

Let us thank the star,
For the brightness,
The constellations,
And the loveliness in the sky.

Reyca Uchiyama (10)
Buxlow Preparatory School, Wembley

Where Shall I Go?

Shall I go to a desert?
Where I can ride a camel.

Shall I go to the Arctic?
Where I can see a polar bear.

Shall I go to Switzerland?
Where I can ski all day.

Shall I go to Australia?
Where I can see kangaroos jump.

Shall I go to France?
Where I can go to Disneyland.

Or shall I go back home
Where I'll be safe and sound?
Where I can be with my friends and family
More fun than any place else.

Mohit Tandon (9)
Buxlow Preparatory School, Wembley

The Head Teacher

There is a head teacher,
Who scares me to death.
When she's around nobody moves,
And nobody takes a breath.

There is a head teacher,
Who sends a shiver up my spine.
And she gives you detention slips,
Which your parents have to sign.

There is a head teacher,
She frightens children away.
She tortures children far and wide,
And she never lets them play.

There is my head teacher,
Who is kind as kind can get.
I shouldn't be too happy,
I haven't seen the substitute yet.

Faadil Patel (9)
Buxlow Preparatory School, Wembley

Friends

I know that it's wrong of me,
But yet I must admit,
When someone doesn't play with me,
I feel like having a fit.

I only have one special friend,
Who is loyal to me,
I always get teased,
Because he is my teddy.

If I could have a real friend,
I would be as happy as can be,
As long as that friend,
Would always stay by me.

Soraya McGinley (10)
Buxlow Preparatory School, Wembley

At The Fairground

At the fairground sounds surround me,
Suddenly I feel so free.
I feel like I could run and play,
I wish I could stay at the fairground all day.

Lights are flashing,
Bumper cars are crashing.
The merry-go-round spins,
Just like whirlwinds.

Children scream and shout,
Everyone is running about.
I felt dizzy and sick,
Like someone had given me a kick.

The music of the merry-go-round plays
And I feel like I'm in a daze.
The rollercoaster soars high,
And then it dives.
Children's faces beam,
This fairground is a child's dream.

Angharad Morgan (10)
Buxlow Preparatory School, Wembley

What Is A Poem?

What is a poem I hear you say?
Well this is what it is.
A poem is a ship to sail to the end of the world,
A poem is a beach with sunbathers and children in the water,
A poem is a desert island with nothing but palm trees and sand,
A poem is a clown, a ghost, a sinking ship,
Anything from land, sea or air,
Or maybe if you even dare you could go beyond.
With so many poems to explore,
Who knows what you will find.

David Cruickshank (10)
Buxlow Preparatory School, Wembley

Books

Books take you far and away,
Books keep your imagination at play,
Books have wonderful things to say,
Books are there for you to read everyday.

Different stories dance in your head,
You can read them in your room, in your bed,
About cats that sing, dogs who dance, all waiting to be fed,
There goes an arrow slaying the dragon down dead.

Fictions of witches, who fly on their brooms in the moonlight,
Two unicorns struggle to have a fight.
Three peacocks fan; what a beautiful sight,
Fireworks bang on a dark, dark night.

Tales of popcorn, candy floss given in the fair,
Children shouting with glee in the air.
Girls playing truth or dare,
Old men giving toddlers a scare.

In my mind skeletons I see,
Princesses, fairies; I smile with glee,
As I close my book gently,
I pull my covers over me.

Another book I'll borrow
Tomorrow . . .

Komal Shah (11)
Buxlow Preparatory School, Wembley

A Shark Experience

Slowly the shark came forward,
Swishing its tail from side to side.
Then I heard a mighty sound,
Which seemed to come from underground.
In the boat I could see a fin that was getting higher and higher,
I realised my mouth was becoming drier and drier!

Soon I could see its head,
Oh, I really wished I was in bed.
Its great white teeth and massive jaws,
So much more menacing than a cat's claws.
Its mouth shut with a big bang,
If it hit me it would have stung!!
I tried to turn the wheel in the boat,
To try and keep myself afloat!

The shark's great body as big as a room,
Threatening me far worse than an old lady's broom!
Once again its huge jaws opened,
I wished it wouldn't munch.
Oh no! . . . *Crunch!*

Vikas Prinja (10)
Buxlow Preparatory School, Wembley

Class Riot

Tim throws a pen in the air,
It slides through Daniel's hair,
The blackboard collapses on the floor,
Bang! Goes the door.
Arnold jumps out the window,
He shouts out 'Nooo.'
Ronald sleeps thinking it's boring,
He's loudly snoring
The teacher shouts out 'Oi!'
Runs up - points at a boy,
His face is red,
He acts as if he's dead.
Harry doesn't look,
And hits Ronald with a book,
The clock goes tick-tock,
Tim got angry and throws the clock,
I throw a bag,
Hits Nicholas and he pretends to sag,
The teacher shouts 'That's it; you all stay in at break!'
Then I jump out of the window and fall in the garden lake.

Mehdi Al-Katib (10)
Buxlow Preparatory School, Wembley

Kill The Homework!

Homework is as bad as bad,
As annoying as can be,
It makes me feel rather sad
When I am told I'm not free!

I hate it rather a lot,
It does so get on my nerves,
It makes me feel very hot,
And I'll have it for years and years!

I always want to get it done,
But sometimes I start it late,
It invades my house like a Hun,
I wish it would stop at some date.

Homework, homework, stop, stop, stop!
Why do you hang over me so?
I wish you'd stop with a plop!
Please, would you just go - please go!

I have to do my homework,
It really makes me not free,
And when I've done my homework,
I'm as happy as can be!

So stop all the awful homework,
I wish it would finish off soon,
The inventor is a great big jerk,
And finish it well before noon!

Roshan Forouhi (9)
Buxlow Preparatory School, Wembley

The Black Rider

The Black Rider's call stings the air like venom
He also is as sour as a lemon
He always rides in darkness and never can be seen
The only thing he eats is a human's spleen.

When he rides it is called the Darkness Hour
He lives right in Death Tower
Armed with a sword with a blade of blood
He buried people alive in the mud.

This monster is a disgrace
To the human race
He is worse than a ghoul
The Black Rider with a black soul.

Alok Prinja (10)
Buxlow Preparatory School, Wembley

When The World Was New

When the world was new,
The birds all happily flew,
The fish all merrily swam,
The sheep cuddled the lamb.
When the world was new,
The plants all joyfully grew,
The chickens laid their eggs,
The cats all licked their legs.
But now the world is old,
And everything is cold,
The cars all honk their horns,
The farmers plough their corn.
But now the world is old,
The people are too bold,
The factories smoke and smoke,
Mechanics fix things broke.
Maybe one day,
The world shall be new again.

Selina Friday (11)
Francis Baily Primary School, Thatcham

Monster Poem

There's a bogey monster,
Coming to get you,
Make sure you hide,
Or he'll blow bogeys all over you.
He's green and gross,
And snotty and grotty,
So watch out for that gruesome bogey monster.

Look under your bed,
There's an ankle grabber!
His fingers are spindly,
His nails are long,
So don't get caught when you get into bed.

Look down your toilet,
There he is!
It's the toilet monster.
His hair is long,

And he has chubby little fingers.
So when you go the toilet,
Watch out!

Katie Dunne (10)
Francis Baily Primary School, Thatcham

Children

Children are disgusting, they're dirty and they smell,
They always moan and cry,
They weep and they yell.
When you need the car for work they always hide your keys,
They always get into mischief and come crying to mummy.
Children are spoilt and get their own way,
And you always have to do whatever they say!

Belinda Sullivan (11)
Francis Baily Primary School, Thatcham

Poor Old Cinderella!

Poor old Cinderella,
She's always cleaning the cellar,
Her mother bosses her about,
The silly old trout,
Poor old Cinderella!

Her fat old sisters,
Gave her blisters,
By her running around,
Not making a sound!
Poor old Cinderella!

Now little Cinders got an invite,
To a party that very night!
As you know, she got a man
Prince Charming - otherwise known as Dan,
Lucky old Cinderella!

They got married, the lucky old things,
The couple exchanged gold rings!
As old Cinders and Danny lived happy,
Her sisters lived in the palace changing the baby's nappy!

Abbie O'Neill (11)
Francis Baily Primary School, Thatcham

Hold On

Hold on if time is letting go
Hold on if it's the last thing that you know
If you fall look inside, you will see there is nothing wrong
Just remember next time that you should hold on.

Hold on if you feel you're losing grip
Hold on or you will fall or maybe trip
If you fall look inside you will see there's nothing wrong
Just remember next time that you should hold on.

Sam Lamden (11)
Francis Baily Primary School, Thatcham

Is There Anyone Out There?

Is there anyone out there?
All the way in outer space.
Is there anyone out there?
Living in that better place.

Is there anyone out there?
Finding their way around.
Is there anyone out there?
Not making a single sound.

Is there anyone out there?
Living in my dream,
Is there anyone out there?
Not having a single team.

Is there anyone out there?
Far above the sky,
Is there anyone out there?
Up so very high.

Is there anyone out there?
Trying to find their way,
Is there anyone out there?
Playing all night and day.

Is there anyone out there?
So very far away.
Is there anyone out there?
That we don't know today.

Is there anyone out there
Collecting a lot of food
Is there anyone out there?
Not getting in a mood
Is there anyone out there?

Chris Halfacree (11)
Francis Baily Primary School, Thatcham

Obnoxious Harry

There once was a prince called Harry,
Who decided he wanted to marry.
So the king declared
'Get everything prepared
For my son to choose who he will marry.'

Many came from far away
To win his love on this special day.
But for everyone the prince would just cry
'I don't like her eye!'
Or 'Ugh! Take it away.'

So this went on for a long time
And made the prince sour as a lime.
After a while
He declared the ladies vile
And told them to go away.

The ladies were appalled at this horrific act
So one of them gave him a smack
Harry was so annoyed
He toyed
With the idea of not getting married!

But then one day a lady came who he liked
And her name was Lady Riked.
But when he asked her to marry him
She said she'd rather marry the bin!
And she wasn't lying!

After this nobody wanted to marry
Prince Harry
Prince Harry of course was very distressed
And refused to dress
For everyone!

Rebecca Petrie (10)
Francis Baily Primary School, Thatcham

I Wish, I Wish!

I wish, I wish I could fly so high
Right above into the sky.
I wish, I wish there was no more school
So I wouldn't have to go to the swimming pool.

I wish, I wish I was an angel above
Just flying about like a dove.
I wish, I wish I was in outer space
But then again it's an empty place.

I wish, I wish I was a crocodile
Swimming about in the Egyptian Nile.
I wish, I wish I was a queen
So regal and squeaky clean.

I wish, I wish it could snow
So it would stop the river flow.
I wish, I wish life was so simple
And the world was the size of a dimple.

I wish, I wish . . .

Meghan Adey-Butt (11)
Francis Baily Primary School, Thatcham

The Country Flowers

The bluebells sing
While the daffodils ring
To a tune of a golden sound.
They frown when in the winter
And smile when in the spring
When the sun is shining
The flowers start to play
And when the rain is pouring
They start snoring.
That is the story of
The country flowers.

Amber-Louise Cockman (10)
Francis Baily Primary School, Thatcham

Spring

I woke up to a lovely spring morning,
Hoping all I could hear is birds singing.
The sun was glimmering with all its might,
Letting us receive its wonderful light.
I could hardly bare to leave the window,
But I knew very well I had to go.
On my way down I let in the fresh air,
As I was wondering what to wear.
I went down to find my mum spring-cleaning,
Because the cobwebs were covering the ceiling.
I ran outside and headed for the park,
As I was running I heard the singing of a lark.
My friend took a camera to photo the birds,
Some were so lovely we ran out of words.
As I realised it was getting late,
I decided to leave my mate.
As my friend went a different way,
I was remembering the joys of my day.
When I got home dinner was almost done,
But I was more interested in which team had won.
The best season really is spring,
Because of all the happiness it brings.

Elouise Clancy (10)
Francis Baily Primary School, Thatcham

Wicked Week

Mad Monday, Mum makes me eat a morning meal.
Terrific Tuesday, Tom tells tots they're terrible.
Worrying Wednesday, Will wishes we weren't working.
Thinking Thursday, Tom thinks too much.
Freaky Friday, Fred eats fish fingers.
Sleeping Saturday snowing saying . . . zzzzz
Studying Sunday, seeing some more science SATs.

Arran Gothard (10)
Francis Baily Primary School, Thatcham

Once Upon A Fairy Tale

My nan said I've got a vivid imagination.
But I'm telling you this is true.
If you don't believe in fairy tales,
Well please don't read on.

When I was in the woods
I saw a door, this door was very old.
It stood quite still, well obviously,
But behind it was just the wood.

I decided to go through the door
And what I saw was truly amazing
It was not normal I say this
Because have you ever seen 'Rapunzel in the woods?'

I saw Peter Pan,
With Tinkerbelle right beside him.
I saw the Hunchback,
And with him, Esmeralda.

As I got closer I realised where I was.
I was in Fairy Tale Land, where else would I be?
Because all these characters have to live somewhere!
Then I had a fright.

I saw the wolf from Riding Hood.
Then I got very worried.
It was getting extremely dark
Where would I go?

Then I saw the good witch from the Wizard of Oz.
And in a zap, there I was back home in the woods.
As I walked back home I realised something strange.
I heard a noise calling my name.

As I looked back I saw Peter Pan
'Hey!' he called, 'You forgot your pink bag.'

Melissa Kenah (11)
Francis Baily Primary School, Thatcham

Fairy Tales

Robin Hood and his Merry Men,
Hiding in their cheerful den,
Robbing from the rich, giving to the poor,
He's a strange hero that's for sure.

'Let down your hair' called the prince
Rapunzel replied 'It needs a rinse'
Then it needed to be dried
The poor prince he tried and tried.

Then dear old Mother Hubbard
Did fill her cupboard
To come back and find . . .
Oh never mind.

Cinderella lost her shoe
What was she going to do?
She cried in the cellar
Poor old Cinderella.

The Billy Goats Gruff
Looked very tough
They laughed with glee
'Cause the troll lost his tea.

The Three Bears sat down to dine
Only Little Bear's porridge was fine
Goldilocks was given some scares
By the Three Bears.

Effie Pearson (11)
Francis Baily Primary School, Thatcham

Sweets, Sweets And More Sweets

My friend eats a lot of sweets
She's got to explode soon.
I say to her 'Stop eating, stop now!'
But she never listens to me.

My dad eats a lot of sweets
He buys and buys.
I say to him 'Stop eating, stop now!'
But he never listens to me.

My mum hates sweets
She doesn't buy a single packet.
I say to her 'Why don't you like sweets?'
She just says 'I don't know.'

My sister loves sweets
She eats until she bursts
I say to her 'Stop eating, stop now!'
But she never listens to me.

My nanny eats a lot of sweets
She eats and eats.
I say to her 'Stop eating, stop now!'
But she never listens to me.

My grandad hates sweets
He can't bear the sight of them.
I say to him 'Why don't you like sweets?'
He just says 'I don't know.'

I love sweets I eat and eat
I can't stop eating sweets
They say to me 'Stop eating, stop now!'
I suppose it's because I'm a sweetie!

Emma Bosher (11)
Francis Baily Primary School, Thatcham

Animals

They come in all different sizes, large or small,
Some are big, and some are tall.
However they come, they are equal to each other,
Some may be adults or babies with their mothers.
They might like the rain, or they might like the heat,
Some are herbivores, some eat meat.
It could be they live in the wild,
Or some might be domestic, timid and mild.
No animal looks totally identical,
They could have patterns, some symmetrical.
Maybe some have sharp, filed claws,
Or large, gaping jaws.
They can be all around us,
Some could be in the train or on the bus.
Always treasure and respect our fellow creatures
Look after them, and observe their amazing features.

Laura Slater (11)
Francis Baily Primary School, Thatcham

Lost Star

Crisp snow is falling on the frosty ground
Not making a sound
Maybe a lost star will be found.

A star floating down to Earth
It may bring us mirth
As it lands on the white turf.

Round and round the snowflakes fall
Maybe no star will fall at all
Because the sky is too tall
And I am too small
To reach.

Gemma Piper (10)
Francis Baily Primary School, Thatcham

Popular Toff

There was a teacher called Mr Toff
He taught at Meffot School,
Every time he taught a class
The girls didn't listen at all.

'Mr Toff,' said a girl called Meghan,
'Don't get me wrong please sir,
But do you have a girlfriend?
If you haven't then I'm her.'

Poor Toff was getting a bit fed up
Being crowded by girls all day,
Then he had a brilliant idea,
Why didn't he run away?

He packed his bags until they were full
(Not forgetting his stash of Snickers).
'Oh no,' he cried, 'I must go back
I've forgotten my pink frilly knickers!'

So back he went with all his bags
He packed his knickers all neat
He tried to find a home near the sewers
But the smell was not too sweet!

He tried a flat, big mistake
His neighbours just read books.
'I want to go back to school.' he whined
So he decided to change his looks!

Hair greased back, thick rimmed glasses
Painted pimples on his cheek,
All the girls never bothered him again
They just ran away and shrieked!

Ellie Bradshaw (10)
Francis Baily Primary School, Thatcham

I Dream

I dream I could fly so high and touch the clouds,
Soft, white and fluffy.
I dream I could meet God and become His messenger,
I would be loyal and friendly.

I dream I had a singing voice like an angel,
Sweet, quiet and calming.
I dream I could dance all day,
Swaying to the sweet music.

I dream the world would turn and become paradise,
All nations at peace.
I dream I could be a superstar,
I would shine in my glory.

I dream I could glow all day,
In the gleaming sun.
I dream I could lie on the beach,
In the soft golden sand.

I dream of health and happiness,
For my family.
I dream of unbroken friendships,
Smiles, fun and laughter.

I dream of freshly fallen snow,
I would shout with joy.
I dream lots of different things,
But will they come true? Maybe one day.

Nicola Gries (11)
Francis Baily Primary School, Thatcham

Snakes

Snakes live in the trees,
They don't have to pay any fees.
Sid has lots of fun,
Out in the sun,
Slithering around peoples' knees.

Snakes are wonderful things,
They have no scaly wings.
They don't need to fly,
It's not fun in the sky, so
Snakes are wonderful things.

Snakes don't have any hair,
They're all very slimy and bare.
No worries about fleas,
Or mean stinging bees,
So they can have fun at the fair.

Snakes eat tonnes of mice,
They think they're very nice.
They won't eat their greens,
Or cheese or baked beans,
Definitely no curry and rice!

Snakes don't like glass tanks,
Or big ships with wooden planks.
They'd rather stay on dry land,
Or in the desert sand,
A car ride, no thanks!

If I were a snake,
I'd make my home near a lake.
Sunbathe all day,
From November till May,
And the rest of the year I'd eat cake!

Charlotte Pascoe (10)
Francis Baily Primary School, Thatcham

School

School is alright, it's just boring,
Chewing a toffee,
While the teacher drinks coffee.

You only do a bit of sport
If you're new don't shirk, be alert.

School is alright, it's just boring,
Chewing a toffee,
While the teacher drinks coffee.

Stay out of sight,
Hide behind the chairs,
Skive if you have to,
But . . . beware!

You'll miss the IT, the fun
And the games, football, spellings
And funny history names.

Don't be a fool,
Don't miss school,
Because . . .

School is alright, it's not boring,
It's just great!

Alex Paddick (10)
Francis Baily Primary School, Thatcham

Love Has An Effect On Our Teacher

When our teacher fell in love with the doctor
She was ill every day of the week.
When she fell in love with the plumber
Her radiator sprang a leak.
When she fell in love with the dustman
She put her bin out every day.
When she fell in love with a farmer
She spent the weekends bailing hay.
When she fell in love with the librarian
She was always borrowing books.
When she fell in love with the policeman
She went chasing after crooks.
But when another teacher
Took our teacher's attention.
They got married straight away
And kept each other in detention.

William Eales (11)
Francis Baily Primary School, Thatcham

River

Slowly and quietly trickling down the moors and hills
Hoping to one day be the sea, all bold and brave.
Going past the hunters and blowing their horns
Like they own the countryside.
The river by now was eroding at the banks
Getting closer and closer every meander to the sea.
Hearing the wedding the distance jolly and cheerful music
Slowly the sound dying away like a plant dying in the winter.
Coming up to the forest with the moonlight shining through the trees
And the light shining on the river like ice.

Bradly Watson (11)
Hildenborough CE Primary School, Tonbridge

Colours Of Day

Bluebells
Are
Blue.
Roses
Are
Red.
Buttercups
Are
Yellow.
Tree leaves
Are green.
Daisies
Are
White.
Tree bark
Is
Brown.
The sky
Is
Bright blue.
All of these
Things are
Colourful.
Colourful.

Chloe Knight (9)
Hildenborough CE Primary School, Tonbridge

At The Mention

At the mention of winter I think of:
The cold bitter winds,
Thinly sprinkled snow,
The icicles hanging as if they will never go,
The bare trees facing storms without fear,
But when the snow melts, the ice disappears I will know that spring
is near.

At the mention of spring I think of:
Baby lambs skipping,
Snowdrops waiting to be found,
Tiny green shoots poking above the ground,
New buds showing, delicate petals on a cherry tree,
When summer is coming those petals will fall just you see.

At the mention of summer I think of:
Flowers in full bloom,
Being down on the beach, chasing the tide,
Looking in rock pools, watching the seagulls glide,
Ripe juicy fruit and rich green leaves on the trees,
And when the leaves turn then autumn it will be.

At the mention of autumn I think of:
Swirling twirling leaves,
They are yellow and orange, not green anymore,
The wind blows them in when I open the door,
The trees are all bare but they're sleeping not dead,
Autumn is ending and winter's ahead.

Louise Whitehead (9)
Hildenborough CE Primary School, Tonbridge

Bugs

Two legs, six legs,
Maybe even eight legs.
Green ones, blue ones,
Lots and lots of shiny ones.
Big ones, small ones,
Also very vicious ones.
Some are fat
And some are skinny.
Some are jumpy,
Some are itchy, also very nippy.
I like bugs.
There are furry and fuzzy ones
And some very, very buzzy ones.
Also very muddy ones.
Bugs!
They all come and see me in my garden
And if they don't I go find them!

James Fullbrook (9)
Hildenborough CE Primary School, Tonbridge

River

Trickle, trickle, splish, splash, splosh
On the move in the grove,
Splosh, bang, bang goes a gun, following the fox on the run
Ripple, trickle, past the chocolate coloured chapel.
Darkness falls over the celebrations,
Sprites flit along quickly like trains coming into stations.
I rush down steep hills filling puddles to the brim.
Inside the castle they're singing a royal hymn.
As I flow out to the sea I think it's a new life for me!

Megan Terry (11)
Hildenborough CE Primary School, Tonbridge

River

Calmly, softly, sweetly it flows
Joining up with others to make it large.
Rippling, bubbling on it goes.
The music plays the river bubbles then it goes around the bend.
Still it carries on its journey to the sea.
Still going, it goes into the forest,
Scarily, creeping along the river comes back into the daylight.
Rushing, gushing on it goes.
Past the castle down the waterfall.
Crash! Through the rapids, over the second waterfall
Knowing that he's nearly there.
Then he suddenly sees where he has to go,
Hurrying he knows the sun is setting
The river's winding he's made it by nightfall.
Now the moonlight shines on it
Like a spotlight shining on the stage which is the river.

Lauren Patience (10)
Hildenborough CE Primary School, Tonbridge

My River

My river starts off as a babbling pool.
My river is very elegant.
It catches up with the hunt to catch a gift.
My river is going to a party so he stops and dances with the wind.
My river is caught in the moonlight
So he looks up and is nearly blinded.
My river is very brave
And is battling with the strong rapids and waves.
My river is coming to an end now; he is not a babbling pool anymore.
My river stops and looks over the hill,
There he sees the place where he belongs.

Becky Broad (10)
Hildenborough CE Primary School, Tonbridge

Story Of River

Splash, splosh, splish, trickle, soft, calm, quiet, gentle.
It swerves from its starting point.
Two more collide with it, on and on,
Horses it sees and hounds with saliva dripping from their mouths.
Something with a sort of black branch is in sight,
I move away quickly, it looks like danger.
I hear bells and tapping,
It's not rain but figures like the man in red except dancing.
It gets dark, the moon almost blinds me with a glow,
Powerful enough to kill.
Suddenly I lose some of my body, I can't control it,
Falling, falling, gone and I never see it again.
Awoken, I hear trumpets, so loud it nearly deafens my ears,
Wait a minute, I hit a rock, I'm splitting, I can't move.
I reach the ocean.
I can't control myself now,
I'm looking back at where I started and say,
I'll see you again just as long as the sun doesn't shine.

Jed Welland (10)
Hildenborough CE Primary School, Tonbridge

The River

Slow and calm trickles and bumps flowing round and down.
Getting faster the river going on its way
Passing softly underneath the canopies of trees
Along goes the river.
Night falling the river dark and magical.
Splash, the river going down a rapid
Bang, crash, slam over rocks fighting everything in its path.
The river almost at an end
For soon it shall be a part of the big wide sea.
The sea is in view closer, closer.
Bang! The river is now a small drop in the sea.

Andrew McNamara (10)
Hildenborough CE Primary School, Tonbridge

River Journey

Trickle, drip, splish, drop, flash, tinkle.
Channel slowly making its way
Erode bend, falling water,
Slosh, splish, cool, grassy stealthy fresh
Wildlife flowing, quiet, peaceful
Grassy, relaxing, green, eco-friendly, graceful.
Splash!
Meander, rush, gush, zooming, frothing,
Bubbling gushing, tumbling, washing, waving,
Wider streams, melodies flowing, harmony,
Salty, zooming,
Almost there, reaching out,
Washing, tumbling, flowing, rumbling, faster, fast, closer, closer
Splash!

Toby Richards (10)
Hildenborough CE Primary School, Tonbridge

The River's Life

Fluent, tingle, soft, calm, gentle, trickle.
Sparkly, magical, swish.
Flowing. Sway, still, slow, quiet.
Fast, quick, ripple, strong, rushing, loud.
Bubbly, noisy, scary, energetic, overflowing, rough, tough, speedy.
Lively deafening, *alive!*
Peaceful, mild, retiring, meek, weakness.
Fizzle out, pass away.
Droop, dwindle, fade.
Disappear! End! Vanish!

Stephanie Ochmann (11)
Hildenborough CE Primary School, Tonbridge

Home Alone

Here I am, I'm home alone,
I'm sitting on the sofa, watching TV.
But the sounds I'm hearing are bothering me
A creak on the stairs, what can it be?
I'm too scared to go and see.
A gurgle in the pipes, it's the heating I know
But my imagination is making me so . . .
Scared!
Still sitting on the sofa, watching TV,
But I've turned it up louder so that maybe
I won't hear those peculiar sounds
That I never notice when people are around,
Scared to move, I'm home alone,
Ding, dong. 'Hi Suzanna, Mummy's home!'
Hooray!

Suzanna Richards (10)
Hildenborough CE Primary School, Tonbridge

The River's Journey

Slosh, splash, splosh, spit, sprinkle.
The river starts and ends there.
It's a child and grows into an adult.
It always lives, it never dies.
It doesn't belong here,
It belongs there, the sea.
It is a beautiful river
When the moon shines through the tree it is also a useful river.
It will one day end up in the sea, never up a tree.
One day the river will love the sea,
The river goes through many places like the trees and the sea.
When the river goes into the trees it feels like it is already in the sea.

Richard Tang (10)
Hildenborough CE Primary School, Tonbridge

The River's Journey

Trickily, tingly, bubbly, rocky, playful flowing calm but happy,
Growing like a child.
Big and grand, horses and hundreds of hounds,
It's joyful and it's dancing around.
But night soon comes,
It's spooky, old, yet magical and mystical.
It's soft and it's gentle too.
It's woody but there's running,
There's fear, the rapids are near.
Splashing and splashing
Playful but there's tension and screams.
The river in all its glory
It's powerful and it's almighty
Its life is over, its journey is at an end.
For it is coming to its home.
Never to see the grass again,
Never to see another tree or slash or splosh
Over the mountainside or meander slowly across a field.
But it's home at last back to the sea, its life's goal completed.
The sea is every bit as grand as the river and every bit as playful
But there is one thing, the sea is not a river.

Jenny Taylor (11)
Hildenborough CE Primary School, Tonbridge

The River

Trickles, trip and stumble into the river.
Then it gets bigger and flows down and down.
Then a foxhunt with people honking horns.
Then the river bounces as people dance and stamp like elephants.
The spotlight of the moon touches the river gentlly.
Then there is a mad scramble as the river goes down rapids.
Then a castle and the river goes faster, burning with jealousy.
Then the river goes to the sea,
And it knows it's going to a better place.

Stephanie Mortlock (11)
Hildenborough CE Primary School, Tonbridge

My River

My stream starts off as a bog,
It will get through every log.

My stream is swift,
It will find its way through the mist.

My stream is getting bigger,
By now it must be a river.

My river is elegant,
Nothing like an elephant.

My river is joining the sea,
I hope it will never forget me.

Sam Thompson (11)
Hildenborough CE Primary School, Tonbridge

The River

The river is always flowing.
No stopping just keeps on going.
Shimmering, splashing, sloshing.
At the start very slow,
But getting faster, here we go.
Gushing, graceful, grand,
There's no knowing
Where we're going.
Just got to find the sea.
Jumping, jolly, jabbering.
But I'm very useful you know.
I'm not just there for show.
Just got to go round the bend,
Towards my journey's end.

Rebecca Moir (10)
Hildenborough CE Primary School, Tonbridge

My Dad And Me Went Boating

My dad and me went boating,
To catch some yummy fish,
So we got our rods and caught one,
And had it for a dish!

Once we'd had our dinner,
We got our sleeping bags out,
But sadly we'd put our rods away,
When we saw a scrumptious trout!

Once we were in our beds,
We read our fishing books,
After that I went to sleep,
And dreamt I was Captain Hook!

Finally it was the morning,
We could tell it had definitely rained,
But sadly we had to go home,
And I hope we will go there again!

Dominic Walkling (10)
Hildenborough CE Primary School, Tonbridge

The River

The river is silent.
The river is loud.
The river is soft.
The river is gentle.
The river trickles.
The river gushes.
The river is out of control when it passes through the rock.
The river glows in the moonlight.
The river bubbles.
The river has rapids,
That tumble toward the sea

Emily François (10)
Hildenborough CE Primary School, Tonbridge

The River

The river starts off as a tiny baby,
A trickle of water gently bubbling happily over rocks and stones,
Getting bigger all the time.
It's getting faster and wider so gradually.
It's growing bigger and bolder, faster and older.
Jumping over rocks and boulders,
Plants and bumps,
Gushing around making waves.
It's becoming less innocent by the minute,
Coming closer towards the sea.
Now it is a fully grown river that has finally finished
It's come down from the mountains.

Caitlin Witcomb (10)
Hildenborough CE Primary School, Tonbridge

Thunder And Lightning

When the storm rages up,
The gale threatens with rain,
But don't forget the lightning
That strikes out of the blue.

The whipping of its tail,
The growth of its branch,
Flash! And then it's gone,
Now the thunder's turn.

It cracks through the air,
Ear-piercing the hearers,
The unbearable loudness,
Rumbles on and goes.

Then the storm calms down,
Hides away for later,
But the lightning will strike again,
Before the thunder explodes.

Charlie Richardson (10)
Hildenborough CE Primary School, Tonbridge

The River

Slowly and soft trickles and bold
Gentle and smooth, splashing and cold.
Flowing and fast bumpy and prancing
Waterfall and rapids hunting and dancing.

Trickling under the trees droplets on the ground
Flowing fast then slow charging along and around.

Streaming, bubbling, quiet and blue.
The river's so fast whoever knew.

Slowly dancing getting faster and faster,
Trickling under the trees. The river's your master.

Tumbling, grand, bouncing and bold.
Getting bigger and bigger the river is old.

Kate McBride (10)
Hildenborough CE Primary School, Tonbridge

The River's Journey

Calm, splash, slow,
Bubbly, shallow, splosh,
Easy flowing, uplifting quiet, gentle,
Relaxing, creative, soft, still.
Light makes me sleepy,
Rushing, speedy, noisy and loud.
Spookily as it bends so fast, quick.
Down the river fast as a car on the motorway,
Rough like two boys fighting tough like they won't give up.
Energetic like a dog, grand and great.
Inviting the river to flow into the sea where it belongs!

Pippa White (11)
Hildenborough CE Primary School, Tonbridge

The Eagle

Swooping through the purple white marshmallow mountains
Ponds far below me iced over with a crystal glaze
The floor of the world littered with flour
Spiky fir trees like iced spiders
My feathered wings glide through the cool, crisp, night air
My beak is the colour of 1000 fires
The clouds around me are as cold as ice
The cool, calm, silent, atmosphere calms me
And I hover over the log cabins below me
That look like they are made out of gingerbread,
And the cattle, sheep and shepherds on the hills
Look like tiny porcelain dolls house figures.
It's getting light I must fly back to my nest
My nest is like a warm tree house
Made out of dental and candyfloss,
With my children inside that are fluffy and small
Like tiny pompoms, cushions and pillows,
All tweeting for juicy crunchy field mice the colour of corn.
Their little beaks open wide
With pink bobbly tongues inside like tiny worms!
Oh how I love the world!

Philippa Edwards (10)
Hildenborough CE Primary School, Tonbridge

Melting Snow

As the snow falls through the air
I stand there watching as it falls into my hair.
And a blanket of white forms on the field
A group of boys make a snowman with a plastic sword and shield.

The sun comes up and melts the snow away
And an end comes to that snowy day.
All the boys heave and groan
And even I give a little moan.

Ben Wood (9)
Hildenborough CE Primary School, Tonbridge

I Love Sport

I love sport, it keeps you fit,
You have to work hard and get into it.

There are three sports I like the best.
I find them better than the rest.
Swimming, running and team netball,
Which is the best? I like them all.

I go like a fish when I swim in the pool.
The speed that I go makes me feel really cool.
Splishing and splashing, I kick and I dive,
Swimming for clubs makes me feel so alive.

Throwing and passing the ball down the line.
My friend scores a goal and it's just in time.
With a shout and a run, a pass and a catch,
I play with my team in a netball match.

My dad and I we love to run,
When we do we have lots of fun.
We jog along at a steady pace,
Sometimes we sprint and have a race.

I love sport, it keeps you fit,
You have to work hard and get into it.

Lauren Goodchild (9)
Hildenborough CE Primary School, Tonbridge

The River

I saw a wedding and the bride, groom and guests
Were doing a dance called the Polka.
The music was very chilling and certainly made me smile.
I look over the castle to see the river,
It is trickling and it was very glistening.
I was watching the fox hunting as they were honking their horns.
The spotlight of the moon glistening like diamonds in the water.
I hear the birds singing with jealousy.

Lauren Humble (10)
Hildenborough CE Primary School, Tonbridge

A Wet And Windy Day

I long for spring on this
Wet and windy day.

The days are too short
On this cold and winter day.

No one out to play on this
Wet and windy day.

The trees are bare and stark
The clouds are grey and dark.

Where is the spring?
Where is the sun?

I long for spring
For spring I long.

Daniel Denton (9)
Hildenborough CE Primary School, Tonbridge

The River

Drip, drip, drip, drip,
Splash, splash, splish, splish.
This is where the river begins,
A trickle of water in the morning.
It passed a hunt growing in pace.
It passed a marriage taking place.
Through the forest past the sprites.
Then came the rapids into sight.
Splashing, swirling,
Twisting, twirling,
Every movement gathering speed
Past a castle, proud and tall
Into the calmness of the sea.

Felix O'Leary (11)
Hildenborough CE Primary School, Tonbridge

Elephants

My favourite animal is an elephant
In pictures they look so cute
I would just love to adopt one
Or keep a baby one in my boot

But one day I heard an elephant
Stomping around next door
I thought I heard it stamping on tables
And making holes in the floor

I thought I heard it drinking bath water
And crashing the kitchen sink
I thought I heard the scream of their daughter
Running past the sink

I thought I heard it in the garden
Squashing all the flowers
I thought I heard it crush the fence
Oh no! The flowers were ours

Stamping around the garden
The elephant went
Standing in the flower beds
Oh! I hope that wasn't meant.

Amy Coles (9)
Hildenborough CE Primary School, Tonbridge

The Wild Rose

I am the queen whom everybody knows;
I am the English Rose;
As light and free as any Jenny Wren,
As dear to Englishmen,
As joyous as a robin redbreast's tune,
The scent of air in June.
My buds are rosy as a baby's cheek,
I have one word to speak,
One word which is my secret and my song,
This is England, England, England all day long.

Jenny Hughes (9)
Hildenborough CE Primary School, Tonbridge

The Wild Rabbit

There he sits his nose a'twitch
Eating grass to fill his tum.

With a hop, skip and a bounce
Over the fence he goes.

His ears are so large
He can barely see, but never mind he still finds his tea.

I wish my rabbit could be tamed
So that I can take him home to play a game.

His ears go back and his eyes go bright
With a hop and a skip he goes home to his burrow for the night.

Alexandra Coles (9)
Hildenborough CE Primary School, Tonbridge

The Caribbean Sea

The Caribbean is so great
It is so fun
It is so hot
It is the place where I want to be
The lovely Caribbean Sea.

And the tortoises are so big,
And the seagulls want their food
It is the place where I want to be
The lovely Caribbean Sea.

And the hotels by the beach
All the luxury that you want
It is the place where I want to be
The lovely Caribbean Sea.

Marc Hawkins (10)
Hildenborough CE Primary School, Tonbridge

A Young Kangaroo From Peru

A young kangaroo from Peru,
Thought it must be a gnu,
It ate leaves and fruit,
Some bamboo and a shoot,
And spent the rest of the day on the loo!

That young kangaroo from Peru,
Decided to eat some hot stew,
It burnt his poor tongue,
Didn't think it was fun,
Now the kangaroo from Peru's gone off stew.

Again that young kangaroo from Peru,
Accidentally fell in a canoe,
Taking a wrong turning at Crewe,
It heard a desolate *moo!*
Which turned out to be a cow that was blue!

Edward Clark (10)
Hildenborough CE Primary School, Tonbridge

Poems Are So Hard

Poems are so hard to write
I really cannot think,
They drive me round the bend
Right up to the brink.

I sit here with an empty mind
No words on the page,
It's really annoying me now
Because my brain just won't engage.

What can I do for my homework?
I just don't have any ideas,
I don't want to do this again
So it definitely won't be my career.

Ross Johnson (10)
Hildenborough CE Primary School, Tonbridge

Pip Squeak

Our guinea pig loves a cuddle,
He closes his eyes and purrs.
He has a long body and twitchy ears,
And a coat of soft ginger fur.

His loving voice squeaks and chatters,
He agrees with me on things that matter.
A bad day is all forgotten,
When I stroke his little bottom.

If I'm worried he reassures me,
By cuddling closer on my knee.
He falls asleep on my lap,
I love to watch him take a nap.

We decided to call him Pip Squeak,
He felt at home within a week.
I feed him beans and broccoli,
But he gives so much more to me.

Eleanor Raishbrook (10)
Hildenborough CE Primary School, Tonbridge

What A Lot Of Nonsense!

It's 8:30pm in the morning,
I can hear the owls calling,
I took off my clothes and got out of bed,
Ate my dinner and scratched my head.
A very old squirrel scampered by,
Stuck out his tongue and caught a fly,
(My cat told me that
While cleaning her hat).
I went to bed the next morning,
And got up the next night,
And then I fell into my attic, what a horrible fright.

Adam Newton (9)
Hildenborough CE Primary School, Tonbridge

What's Unique About Me?

I have a nose for smelling
I have ears to hear
I have a smile to spread happiness
I have eyes to see my family
But everyone has these, so what's unique about me?

I'll tell you what's unique about me
I have special hands to hold my friends
I have a heart as big as a house
I have lots of love to spread around
I am me, me, me!

I have a nose for smelling
I have ears to hear
I have a smile to spread happiness
I have eyes to see my family
But everyone has these, so what's unique about me?

I'll tell you what's unique about me
I have chubby cheeks which people squeeze
I have a laugh unique to me
I have soft and gentle hair
I am me, me, me!

Sophie Worsfold (10)
Hildenborough CE Primary School, Tonbridge

Inspiration

To write a poem you need inspiration,
Which I think I'm the only person who hasn't got it in
the whole nation,
I could write about a dream,
Or a piece of driftwood floating on a stream,
I could write it about a cold and stormy night,
Or a haunted house and give everyone a fright,
I could write about a monster that won't rest,
Or a simple thing like a bird making a nest,
So many things I could do,
But I still do not have a clue.

I could make it long,
Or should I write a short song,
I could make it three lines,
And be done with it in record breaking time,
I could write it about the day in the life of a pen,
Or a nonsense poem about a hen,
I could write it about lions in a jungle,
Or scribble some lines down and make it any old jumble.

I've just noticed something new,
But I don't think it could be true,
I think I've just written a poem
Seriously, I did it without even knowing,
I can't believe I done it at last,
And proved all those things wrong I've said in the past.

Lydia Regis (10)
Hildenborough CE Primary School, Tonbridge

Zephyr

As the wind I have a lot to do
Tickling cows with my breezes until they moo.
Racing round the world fast as any mouse
Blowing through a shack or around the walls of a house.

But I bring good not just bad
My whispered flurries make people so glad.
Diving down towards the desert ground
Scattering dust from a termite mound.

I also bring blizzards and horrible storms
Uprooting trees from well kept lawns.
The worst of my storms are when lightning joins in
Add hail and thunder it's more than a din.

When I'm bored I puff seeds and plant crops
Sending children's kites right to the treetops.
And when the flowers are old and dead
I will make their petals shed.

And as I travel through the sky
I scrape the flesh off those who die.
Puffing leaves from freshly swept piles
Scattering seeds for miles and miles.

Soaring and gliding through the air
It's always me, I'm always there.
You could search for eternity to find me
Though I'm the flight of a feather or a rustle of a tree.

Flo Simpson (9)
Hildenborough CE Primary School, Tonbridge

Snow

Snow is like a scattered jewel,
Sparkling on the icy pool.
Children skate without a care,
But really they should beware.

When the snow comes it is bitter,
Up the road comes the gritter.
Spreading salt onto the ground,
People peep out to hear the sound.

They wrap up warm in gloves and scarves,
And walk along the slippery paths.
Everyone loves a snowball fight,
But you can get a frosty bite.

All the birds will fly away,
Except for the robin who will stay.
The curious kittens leave paw prints in the snow,
As a mark showing you where they go.

Lying on the fluffy snow,
Waving your arms to and fro.
The snow will hold you close in its arms,
Making angels with snowy charms.

It's great to be out when it snows,
But I get cold, my poor toes and nose.
I like to snuggle in my home,
I'm glad I don't live in an icy dome.

Jessica Lipington (10)
Hildenborough CE Primary School, Tonbridge

My Narrow Escapes

I walked down to the sandy shore,
And put my feet into the sea,
But quickly took them out again
When a crab came close to me.

I ran right down the sandy shore,
And dived into the sea,
Narrowly missing a hippo's head -
A lucky escape for me.

I skipped down to the sandy shore,
I fell into the sea.
To see a school of piranha,
Close to eating me.

I legged it down the sandy shore,
And ducked under the sea.
Because a swarm of killer bees
Was chasing after me.

I jogged down to the sandy shore,
And plunged into the sea.
But soon I met a crocodile
That had lain in wait for me.

I jumped down the sandy shore,
And bounced into the sea.
I landed on a shark's head
And that was the end of me.

I walked again down the sandy shore,
At the age of just eleven.
But nothing could harm me any more
Because *I* was now in Heaven.

James Plimmer (9)
Hildenborough CE Primary School, Tonbridge

Frost Bite

I love the different shapes and sizes of icicles,
Hanging like a chandelier from a great ceiling.
Hundreds upon hundreds of tiny diamonds
Like Jack Frost's fingers touching the morning
Spreading their wintry magic.
Perfect patterns of ice cover the trees and rooftops
Like a frosty icing.
Snow starts to fall softly and silently.
New, fresh, untouched, lilac in the winter sun.
I love the way the snow crunches when I walk on it.
I love making snowmen, snow angels
(Even though I'm a little devil) and not forgetting snowballs.
My fingers and nose tingle in the cold air,
My toes go numb and start to pain -
I think that Jack Frost is being naughty playing his icy games again.

Tom Iliopoulos (10)
Hildenborough CE Primary School, Tonbridge

Leopards

Slinking through the tall grass,
Trying to catch her prey,
Waiting for the chance,
For it to run her way.

Running, chasing, pouncing,
Lying ready to jump,
Great! She's got it,
I can hear the bones go crunch.

What! She's seen a hyena.
That's not a good sign,
Great! She ran up that tree,
Just - in - time.

Molly Noble (9)
Hildenborough CE Primary School, Tonbridge

Bump

A man was walking down the road
With his morning cup of tea
When suddenly without warning
He smashed into a tree.

Amazingly he wasn't hurt
And so continued to his car
But it wasn't long before he was,
When he hit an iron bar.

It broke his leg
That's what it did
And so to the hospital he limped
But once again he hurt himself, by tripping on a brick.

Bang! Bump! Crash! Went things
As he bumped across the road, he'd be sorry,
Because halfway across,
He was flattened by a lorry.

He decided to make an appointment, by phoning 'em
On his mobile phone
But the nurse said, 'Sorry we can't help
For you've broken every bone.'

James Tribe (10)
Hildenborough CE Primary School, Tonbridge

Spring

Baby lambs being born,
Buds coming up to greet us
Trees blossoming.

Sunshine coming out with a happy face on.
People smiling all the time.
Birds come back and make a new clean nest to live in
Until winter comes again.

New babies are born,
Proud and excited mothers and fathers.
People living in new homes and having a wonderful time.

People make new starts because spring is coming!

Laura Tolhurst (9)
Hildenborough CE Primary School, Tonbridge

Monsters

Tall monsters, short monsters
Fat monsters, thin monsters
Big monsters small monsters
Monsters, monsters everywhere
Who shall we see today?
Dracula, Frankenstein or even a ghost
Where shall we see them?
Down at the docks up a mountain,
We shall see, shall we see them?
High or low, I don't know.
There's lots of places they can be,
So there's monsters, monsters, everywhere you see.

Liam Kemp (9)
Hildenborough CE Primary School, Tonbridge

The Yearly Visit

'Hurry up' my mother said
'Tidy up and make your beds.'

'Wash your hands and wash your face,
My, my, aren't you a disgrace.

Go and get your best clothes on,
Hurry up, we haven't got long.

Aunt Martha's coming for tea,
Now boys, do you need a wee?

Quickly, quickly put the oven to bake,
While I get the ingredients for the cake.

Oh my, is that the time?
Only five minutes 'til she arrives.

Now boys are you looking your best?
Peter come on, tuck in your vest.

Oh my goodness, here she comes,
Quickly Harry, cover up those crumbs.'

'Hello dears, how was school?
Are you obeying all the rules?

What do you think of my new frock?
How about it, don't I look hot?

I've bought you both some dungarees,
Don't you like them, aren't you pleased?

Well, I must be on my way,
Ta, ta, toodel-oo 'til another day.'

At last the end of the visit is near
I'm glad it only happens once a year.

Rebecca Hird (10)
Hildenborough CE Primary School, Tonbridge

Animals

Birds have wings
And in the sky they soar.
While lions are fierce
With a very loud *roar!*

Fish can swim
And they have scales.
Some sharks are grey,
Just like lots of whales!

Giraffes are big
And they are very tall.
Mice are the opposite
And very, very, very small.

Elephants are huge
And walk with a thud.
Pigs are smelly
And roll in the mud.

Anteaters have long noses
And they eat ants.
Monkeys are intelligent,
But they don't wear pants!

Woodworms are a nuisance
And chew at wood.
But earthworms are pink,
And they do gardeners good.

Rabbits are cuddly
And hop a lot
Unlike leopards,
They have spots.

Oliver Kendall (9)
Hildenborough CE Primary School, Tonbridge

Seasons

Four there are every year
Spring, summer, autumn, winter, hooray!
Winter white, cold and freeze,
Frost and snow makes me sneeze.

Spring harvest, lambs and crops.
Easter in-between chicks and chocs.

Summer is so fresh and free,
Water fights and cooling sodas for free.

Autumn days when the leaves fall,
The animals are going, the people have gone.

Divia Marwaha (9)
Hildenborough CE Primary School, Tonbridge

Crashing Waves

Waves like a great white shark are near.
Boats struggling like a great white shark is swallowing them whole.
Wild wind howling like a wolf.
Rain forming a giant rain cloud.
Baby fish trying to find their mother.
The waves crash on.

Michael Corsini (8)
Hilltop First School, Windsor

The Horrid Sea At Night

The sea glows in the moonlight.
The waves seem to be hungry,
Swallowing up shells like a lion feasting on his prey.
The waves go forwards and backwards
As fast as Concorde flying in the air.

Liam Ainsby (9)
Hilltop First School, Windsor

The Scary Storm

The thunder crashes with the lightning.
Booming thunder as rain falls.
The thunder is crashing against the rain.
The thunder echoes like a giant's clap.
The animals huddling in a spooky cave making howling sounds
Because the spooky thunder is here.
As the thunder goes, the inky black sky arrives.

Hina Jaffri (9)
Hilltop First School, Windsor

The Swirling World

The storm like a roaring lion thumping loudly on the rooftops.
Cold as frozen ice.
Storm's splashing against the window.
When the storm comes you cuddle up in smooth soft fur.
Swirling like a frozen world.
It's like a spying sea.
It's like a swirling spinner.

Andrea Ljungberg (8)
Hilltop First School, Windsor

Lightning Storm

The thunder crackles like an angry tiger running for its prey.
As lightning strikes the dusty ground.
The storm is like an angry wasp from above.
Jack Frost comes as the lightning strikes.
He covers the cars in frost.

Charlotte Harmes (9)
Hilltop First School, Windsor

The Echoed Sea

Seagulls trace the wave's line like a racing car following a track.
Waves crash together creating a white frothy surface.
Seagulls plunge over the fishermen
Booming out scared words without hope.
Fish get disturbed from the peaceful rest.
Seaweed sways like Mexican dancers.
Black sea echoes and ripples the earth.

Alex French (9)
Hilltop First School, Windsor

The Sea And Storm

The waves are crashing together like children clapping their hands.
Tumbling waves seem to bounce over each other
Like children having fun on a trampoline.
Rocks being splashed
Like terrified young children in a swimming pool.

Lucy Greely (9)
Hilltop First School, Windsor

The Deep Blue Sea

Scuba divers descend for exotic fish
The fish racing through caverns in the sea
Going deeper you see rotting boats with fish hiding
The laid back surf gliding onto the shore
Electric eels sending a shock through the waves
Fishermen lost in the blue
People falling off rocking banana boats
Fish darting through the water.

Callum Barrett (8)
Hilltop First School, Windsor

The Banging And Crashing Thunder

The parents rushing to get their children out of the wind and thunder.
The zigzagging lightning whips across the sky.
The lightning crashes loudly and bangs quickly.
The storms whirl around in circles round and round.
The growling and miserable and rumbling rain crashes.
The rocks crack and tumble from cliffs being hit by the hard waves.
The animals growl and try to get in their grey old homes.

Kerry Newman (9)
Hilltop First School, Windsor

A Monday Morning On The Sea

The red hot sun shines on the glittering sea.
Seagulls - begging for food
So they dash down and snatch food off hungry people.
A little boy looks at all the colourful coral in the deep blue sea.
When the tide comes in it washes the sand away.

Kerry Hogg (8)
Hilltop First School, Windsor

Scary Night In Spain

The storm is coming out like a volcano erupting on the rocks.
Lightning crashing on the sea.
Splashing, all the animals fighting for safety.
The dolphins are rushing
Like people trying to get to work in a traffic jam.
The night is as dark as a black furry coat.

Cerise-Kumal Uppal (9)
Hilltop First School, Windsor

The Deep Sea

The waves crash as if they are a cheetah running for its prey.
The waves crash against the rocks as if a lion is angry.
The shiny blue sea is as shiny as a polished shoe.
Fishes swim slowly and gently under the deep sea.

Hamzah Riaz (9)
Hilltop First School, Windsor

The Stormy Sea

The erupting waves smash the edge of the rocks.
The powerful thunder strikes the side of the boat.
The wind forces mini tides that go aboard the boat.
The rain like a massive shower pouring down.

Martin Barnett (8)
Hilltop First School, Windsor

On The Beach

On the beach the sea is all calm
Until all the clouds go grey and it started to rain.
Thunder and lightning come rushing down from the clouds.
All the people are trying to get into their houses
But the waves keep coming on the shore.
It looks like if it is pulling them into the water.
It looked like it was trying to drown them.

Nathan Stevenson (8)
Hilltop First School, Windsor

The Tiger Echoing In The Scary Storm

The tigers are pestering their children trying to get to safety.
Another echo comes from a big, dark, empty space
Dogs shaking like wobbly jelly.
Lightning just like mad and bad tempered fire.
A gust of wind hits me just like a ghost.
A loud crackle comes through, help me, help me, survive!

Stephanie Brench (9)
Hilltop First School, Windsor

The Billowing Sea

The waves charging against the rocky shore like a herd of elephants.
A gigantic dolphin disturbs the mini fish.
A sea urchin appears up above the billowing shore.
The waves crushing the boats like a stone shark.
Wild seagulls swoop past the tranquil shore
Hoping the washy shore flows away from them.

Max Kinsler (9)
Hilltop First School, Windsor

The Stormy Sea

The waves were leaping to the height of the tallest lighthouse.
The crashing waves sound like thunder in the dead of the night.
The fish swimming frantically away from the crashing waves.

Ian Bell (8)
Hilltop First School, Windsor

Stormy Seas

Heavy rains splashing against the silver rocks.
Waves tumbling over the long metal ships.
Bright lightning and thunder bashing and crashing together.
Ships lapping over the smashed rocks.
Clouds covering the moon as fast as a racing car.
The wooden boats all crumbled into little crunchy pieces.

Zoe King (9)
Hilltop First School, Windsor

The Sea In A Storm

The waves are jumping over one another
Like a kangaroo having fun.
The waves are crashing on the rocks
As if they are trying to swallow them up in one go.
Leaping dolphins anxiously hurry to find shelter in the deep, dark sea.

Charlotte Kellet (9)
Hilltop First School, Windsor

The Ups And Downs Of Walking

Putting on your boots, getting some food.
Packing your rucksack, you're in a good mood.
Looking at the mountain, checking the weather.
Now your bag's not as light as a feather!

Trudging through the mud, scaring the sheep.
Climbing the rocks, eating your sweets.
Taking a rest now that you're at the peak.
Look at the view; you could stay here all week.

Tromping back down, telling some jokes.
Walking to the bar, ordering cokes.
Laying down flat, you've injured your knee.
Now you're ready for a big slap-up tea!

Alex Burrell (10)
Oaklands Junior School, Crowthorne

The Fairy Gathering

Dainty legs and
Flowing curls
Tiny toes and
Primrose pearls
Twinkling eyes and
Happy faces
Beauty pageants, running races.

Meeting up and
Saying hello
Waving cheerily and
Some cries of 'No!'
Some little fairies need their beauty sleep,
Leave them alone, let them count their sheep!

Red wings and
Silky hair
Young faces and
Shining frocks they love to wear
Long pretty eyelashes and
Ruby red lips
Daisy chains from head to foot
And diamond rings and candles lit.

Leave them be,
And let them rest
For all you're worth
Outside may be a fairy,
A fairy
A fairy
Seeking your wish.

Sarah Robey (10)
Oaklands Junior School, Crowthorne

Why Are They Looking At Me?

Am I really so wonderful and good looking?
I'll never know,
Some things, humans I think, come and stare.
I sit on my ledge padded with straw
And stare back at them.
Nothing happens.
I try something different.
Oh yes, oh yes, they cheer as I
Reach and swing and grab and jump,
Bounce and pounce and then with a bump,
I sit and tug off the skin of a long, yellow thing,
I don't know what it is but it sure tastes good!
I remember a place,
Where the ropes were vines and the nets were leaves,
Where the faces were mean and evil,
Not smiley and happy.
I ran away but not in time,
I was caught.
I don't know what happened next but all I know is
I am safe and happy,
Swinging, jumping, leaping, scratching, bouncing, pouncing
And eating long yellow things,
I don't know what they are but they sure taste good!

Emma Kennedy (10)
Oaklands Junior School, Crowthorne

The Night

Darkness fills the air with slumber,
In the silence of night.
Children sleeping under blankets,
So quiet and so right.

Adults eating out at dinner,
Eating lots and lots.
Horses taking the adults home.
Trot, trot, trot.

Ella Freeman (10)
Oaklands Junior School, Crowthorne

Circus

'Come to the circus!'
The posters call
Mothers and fathers
Children and all.

The tootle of a horn
On comes the clown.
He climbs a ladder
But falls straight down.

A beautiful girl
On a flying trapeze -
A strong young man
Catches her by the knees.

Here come the animals
The trainer cracks his whip.
The lions roar, the horses jump
And the dogs perform some flips.

The performers come on
They all take a bow
The people all cheer
'Please give us more now!'

Madeleine Burrell (7)
Oaklands Junior School, Crowthorne

The Caribbean Crab

The crab scuttles along the sunny beach
Shining its sparkles in the beaming sun.
Clicking his clackety claws
He scurries into the shimmering sea.

Down there he snaps his claws
At a passing shoal of fish.
Then says hello to his ferocious friends
Before he clickety clacks his way home.

Natalie Thompson (8)
Oaklands Junior School, Crowthorne

My Little Sister

My little sister really makes me laugh,
She splashes the water right out of the bath.
It lands on the floor in a giant puddle,
Mummy comes in and says 'What a muddle!'

My little sister swims like a fish,
But she never eats them served on a dish!
Except for fish fingers, or maybe fishcakes,
Covered in ketchup - what a mess she makes!

My little sister works hard at school,
But when she comes home she plays the fool!
Like when she's reading Harry Potter,
She tends to call him Barry Trotter!

My little sister has a mischievous giggle,
If you hold her too tightly, she'll probably wriggle!
She always has her nose in a book,
She closes it up if you sneak a look!

My little sister is the best there can be,
She never hesitates to play with me.
She's younger than me, I'm older than her,
She thinks she knows best, but I know better!

Stephanie Lovell-Read (9)
Oaklands Junior School, Crowthorne

Snow

On the icy road,
People shiver in the cold.
Our gardens, fields
And hills,
Exist no more.
Instead there is a world of white,
With not a single mark in sight.
Snow, snow everywhere.

Caitlin O'Neill (10)
Oaklands Junior School, Crowthorne

My Rocking Horse

Day in, day out,
My rocking horse will be about.
Day in, day out,
My rocking horse will always help out.

I play with her in the morning,
I play with her in the evening,
I play with her in the afternoon
And braid her silky mane.

The tea bell rings,
The kettle sings,
And off I go,
Rocking to and fro.

Day in, day out,
My rocking horse will be about.
Day in, day out,
My rocking horse will always help out.

I gallop out of the kitchen,
And trot into the garden.
There we play till bedtime
When we canter into dreams.

My rocking horse and I shall never be parted,
My rocking horse and I shall always be friends.
My rocking horse and I shall ride together until the sun is nigh.

Day in, day out,
My rocking horse will be about.
Day in, day out,
My rocking horse will always help out.

Jessica Lehmani (10)
Oaklands Junior School, Crowthorne

The Enchanted Garden

A bird flutters quickly, from tree to tree,
Trying to get home to her little ones,
A squirrel tramps along the lawn, feeling free,
The silence settling him,
The animals see that the snow came thick and crispy,
Like a blank page!

The invisible painter came painting everything white,
He tried not to trudge along the glistening new snow,
The birds and the animals were enjoying this and they watched,
As children peeked out of their windows,
And shouted *'Yippee!'*

The animals slunk away not wanting to play in the cold anymore,
But the little bird sat in the tree like a glowing ember,
Still watching the snow come down,
As the children came out,
She flew away and thought to herself,
This was an enchanting garden, no more.

Bethany Allen (10)
Oaklands Junior School, Crowthorne

Big Bad Literacy

My messy English
Puts Miss Teacher in anguish
A blot here . . .
A smudge there . . .
Punctuation missing everywhere!
You won't find a teacher within a mile
That will look at my handwriting style!

That was the story of a boy
That lived only to annoy
The teacher who will always remember
That start of term in September.

David Lehmani (10)
Oaklands Junior School, Crowthorne

The Tiger

Prowling through the jungle, all of them have names.
This one's name is Bungle, he's playing lots of games
He's just a cub but who cares? He really scares me when he glares!
He's getting a teaching from his dad, his pouncing lessons.
So he'll become a strong lad,
He loves that lesson so he'll learn aggression.
He's not a lion, so he won't grow a mane!
Yet you won't see him down the lane!
He's growing older not a cub at five,
When he was four his head got stuck in a beehive.
When he was three he got stuck in a tree.
When he was two he suddenly shot up and grew!
When he was one I certainly can't tell you the things he's done!

Kate Wood (9)
Oaklands Junior School, Crowthorne

Disaster

Disaster is black.
It hangs over everyone,
Just waiting to fall.

And when it does fall,
There is often tears and fear,
Which are hard to clear.

Disaster springs out,
Of the shadows like a cat,
Scratching happiness.

When disaster springs,
Covered in black, unlucky one,
Happiness is drained.

But disaster goes,
Like everything this day.
Happiness then comes.

Daniel Bean (11)
Oaklands Junior School, Crowthorne

The Deserted Hill

The deserted hill
Where no one goes,
Where there are vultures
As well as crows.

All falls silent,
As quiet as can be,
But something rustles
From behind a tree.

A freezing cold wind
Sweeps through the air,
And the vultures that are feasting
Look up and stare.

A large hooded creature
About two metres tall,
Begins to step forwards,
Careful not to fall.

All of a sudden
The sun starts to rise,
And the air is filled
With deafening cries.

The creature starts screaming,
It falls to its knees,
It starts to dissolve
Vanishing beneath the trees.

That was the story
Of the deserted hill,
Where a creature raided,
But now all is still.

Sam London (11)
Oaklands Junior School, Crowthorne

The Sea Roars

The sea roars, as it crashes against the rocks in its anger.
The sea roars, as it swallows the boats in greed.
The sea roars, as it swirls into whirlpools.
The sea roars, as it searches for things.
The sea roars, and it lurks waiting.
The sea roars, and it moans.
The sea roars, furiously.
The sea roars.

Sophie Stafford (10)
Oaklands Junior School, Crowthorne

Who Am I?

I run like the wind.
If a man can change his stars
I can change my spots
I seek my prey,
I leap and jump,
My prey screams and shouts,
The cows run about.

My wife sometimes seeks,
The cubs like to play,
I live in the zoo
And sometimes the jungle
Who am I? Can you guess?
Shall we give you some more?
My body is the colour of the sun
My spots are so grey they look like they're black.

My claws are so sharp they can slice through your skin,
I roar so loud you cannot hear a thing
Come on, have a guess!
Do you know who I am or do you not?
I am a cheetah the fastest creature on Earth!

Georgia Loft (8)
Oaklands Junior School, Crowthorne

Silence

A clock without a tick,
Shh! Listen it's silence.
A classroom without any children,
Shh! Listen it's silence.
A drum without beaters,
An animal without a voice,
A bed with no one sleeping there,
Shh! That's silence.

A television switched off,
Shh! Listen it's silence.
A lesson with all the children paying attention,
Shh! Listen it's silence.
An airport without people
A runway without planes
An entire planet with no one around
Shh! That's silence.

Charlotte Wain (8)
Oaklands Junior School, Crowthorne

Football Match

I could see the ball flying,
And hear the crowd's cheers dying.
The grass was a shiny carpet,
Spread down on the ground.

I could feel my heart beating heavily,
And see the players dribble cleverly.
The stadium was built so strongly.
Unlike a cub's first step.

I could hear the encouraging calls,
And feel my dad's pulls.
To get me out the way,
So he could see the play!

Robert Tolcher (10)
Oaklands Junior School, Crowthorne

Who Am I?

I smell like a food eater swooping through the air
No one can hear me
Nobody can see me
I hide in my tree up above the shadow of darkness
I lie
My kingdom is below me, this is where I live
North Alaska
My prey is somewhere in the water
If I find it I will dive
My feathers are long and brown,
With claws so sharp I catch my prey
My head is white
People think I'm bald
My beak is sharp
Who am I?
Bald eagle.

Matthew Freeman (7)
Oaklands Junior School, Crowthorne

My Magnificent Rhino

My rhino is silver like the shining grey wolf,
Silver like the shimmering moon in the night sky,
Silver like a twenty-pence coin!
His growl is like an avalanche coming straight down.

My rhino is red like an angry guard.
He is like autumn and spring,
Half of him is orange like a bright sun,
Half of him is like a scaly T-Rex.

My rhino's horn shines in the light,
His tail swishes like a grandfather clock,
His body is a castle wall protecting his kingdom,
He resembles the stars.

William Thompson (11)
Oaklands Junior School, Crowthorne

Hold On

Have you ever got the feeling that something is wrong?
And everyone tells you just to hold on
Well, when it happens to me
I play it in a song and it all happens like this.

I pick up my guitar
Brain racking for words and then suddenly
One thousand words appearing in my brain
My feelings just flowing through my arm and down to the strings
Both slipping out of my mouth,
And slithering across my fingers like a serpent.

Suddenly I've lost control and playing my feelings out in
song and music
After I have no need to shout
I am lost in my feelings and music
I feel happy and sad at the same time
Just like a kite without a string.

A car without wheels,
A face without a name,
But after spilling my feelings
I feel like the breeze!
Free and ever flowing.

Sometimes, my face is a river
Tears plummeting down my face,
But even then I let my feelings free in a sad song
The beat runs through me like my heart pumping,
And suddenly I'm lost in my own little world.

To make me feel happy,
It only takes me,
A beat,
And my guitar.

It's just called holding on.

Jess Turner (10)
Oaklands Junior School, Crowthorne

White Horses

Galloping white horses run across the bay;
The world is frozen on this day,
I step outside,
Boots done up tight,
Some would call this a darkened sight.

The giant waves roll in the last of the light;
There's an army of soldiers riding tonight,
Their spears plunge,
Into the icy depths,
They did this for hours while I slept . . .

A murky grey blur, that's all I see,
I'm hoping to find the great ocean's old key
To reveal the power, the soldiers have yet to confide
All they've done so far; is lied . . .

Maybe tomorrow they'll have gone;
But I know myself the battle
Was never finished
Nor done . . .

Georgina Ross (11)
Oaklands Junior School, Crowthorne

The Weather

The weather, the weather, always changes everyday
Every minute
Sometimes cold, sometimes hot.
Everyday could be warm or cool.
You can't be sure.

I think that it should be warm because that's in-between
It changes faster than a rat can run
It can jump faster than a kangaroo
I like to see the sun
Because then I can get a tan.

Imogen Murray (7)
Oaklands Junior School, Crowthorne

The Easter Bunny

The Easter bunny,
Has big feet,
Floppy ears,
And things you like to eat

He's white and pink,
Has a fluffy tail,
He always delivers,
In snow, sleet or hail!

He runs, he jumps,
He bounces and skips,
Kids everywhere,
Are licking their lips

Everyone loves,
The gifts he brings,
The children laugh,
As he sings.

Olivia Cox (10)
Oaklands Junior School, Crowthorne

Spring

Spring has sprung
The flowers are young
The petals are growing
With the sun glowing
Red and yellow flowers
Sprouting everywhere
Sending their perfume in the air
The birds are nesting
Waiting for their mates
The dogs are resting
By the garden gates
The evening is drawing out
So we need to give a big shout
Welcome in the summer after spring was such a stunner.

Sarah Andrews (8)
Oaklands Junior School, Crowthorne

Roses Are Red

Roses are red
Violets are blue
Nothing is as good
As Christmas and you.

Roses are red
Violets are blue
Spring is here for
You this year.

Roses are red
Violets are blue
Nothing is as sweet
As you.

Roses are red
Violets are blue
Kittens are sweet
Just like you.

Roses are red
Violets are blue
Valentines is special
But not as much as you.

Lisa Field (8)
Oaklands Junior School, Crowthorne

My Brother

He's a spinny whizzy chair,
He's a sparkling yellow door that's always open,
He's a fluffy playing puppy which is barking mad,
He's a strong brave eagle that kicks around a stone
He's a smelly sock which sometimes smells fresh,
The look of excitement when there's a dog around,
A dazzling spark of sun with a lovely lick,
A hot chocolate to calm him down
A cheeky monkey.

Lee Hopwood (10)
Oaklands Junior School, Crowthorne

The Ant

Nobody thinks much of an ant,
Just a plain old ant,
But why do they squash it and say,
'Only an ant'
Maybe an elephant should tread on us and say,
'Only a human'
Is it because they're common?
Dogs are common.
Is it because they're small?
Butterflies are small.
Is it because they're black?
Some cats are black.
Is it because they've got lots of legs?
Octopuses have lots of legs.
Well, why is it then?
Maybe . . .
Maybe what?
Maybe it's all of them.
All of what?
The things . . .
Common, small, black and lots of legs.

Chloe Bentley (9)
Oaklands Junior School, Crowthorne

My Dolphin

Blue like the bright blue sea,
Warm like the shining sunshine.
Its squeaking, slicking sound
As he swims fast along the sea.
As I reach to touch his fin
So smooth but like leather it feels.
All I wish to do,
Is swim alongside him once again.
He is my life,
And always will be.

Gemma Field (10)
Oaklands Junior School, Crowthorne

Droplets Of Rain . . .

I wonder where they're going?
What they're going to find
They bump into each other,
But they don't seem to mind.

Droplets of rain,
Tiptoeing down
The windowpane.

They slide around,
They dance and play
Are those droplets having fun
On a day like today?

Droplets off rain,
Tiptoeing down
The window pane.

They chase around,
Leaving dainty trails
Like that of a snail, but more delicate.
Gliding gracefully, no sound.

Droplets of rain, droplets of rain . . .

Rhiannon Hitt (11)
Oaklands Junior School, Crowthorne

Who Am I?

I am elegant and I live in the deep blue sea
I am silky
I am graceful and I jump between waves.
People love me.
I am a bluey greyish colour although I am still beautiful
People pay lots of money to swim with me
Some people would love to adopt me
Kiss me I squeak
Who am I?

Charlotte Wells (8)
Oaklands Junior School, Crowthorne

My Magic Box

(Based on 'Magic Box' by Kit Wright)

I will put it in my box . . .
The barbarian bark of my first dog,
A petal of a pretty, pleasant poppy,
The blessed breeze of a beautiful winter's day

I will put it in my box . . .
A teacher working at a desk and a child teaching them,
Night being day and day being night,
A dog eating a fish and a cat eating a bone

I will put it in my box . . .
The wish that came true for me,
A peaceful dream of a newborn baby,
The first Christmas bell I ever heard

I will put it in my box . . .
The sinking sun on a summer's night,
A delicate dolphin leaping into the clear blue sky,
The rapid, raging waterfall falling on the rough rocks.
My box is made of gold, silver and bronze from the Olympic Games.
It is fashioned with emeralds, rubies and sapphires all wished for
from a magic genie.

My magic box is going to be locked in my heart and opened at
the end of my time.

Elliott Markham (11)
Oaklands Junior School, Crowthorne

The Alley Cat

The alley cat walks down the streets
Saying anything to those he meets
Then as you try to flee from him
He jumps and makes a terrible din
The alley cat stalks down the streets.

Peter Hitt (9)
Oaklands Junior School, Crowthorne

Snow

The snow is falling,
The ground is getting white,
The children are building snowmen,
Some are having snowball fights,
Snowflakes, snowflakes, kept on falling just for me.
The dogs are running leaving paw marks in the snow,
Birds are sitting in the snow white trees singing their songs,
Snowflakes, snowflakes, kept on falling just for me.

Laura Coppen (8)
Parkway Primary School, Earith

The Child In Me

The child in me wants to grow up and be a lady some day.
The child in me wants to run into the world but is too scared
of the unknown.
My heart races like a tiger chasing its meal.
The child in me wants to play like a puppy.
The child in me wants to be free like a bird but I am only a child.
Wondering if the world is safe or am I in danger of always
keeping it safe.
The child in me wants to dance like a ballerina.
The child in me wants to sing with an open heart.
The child in me wants to be like a lion so I can be strong.
The creativeness of a youth in a world where I can be what I want.
Growing pains of the world in a child's eyes.
What a world, what a child, what a life.
The child in me is as free as a bird.
The child in me is as blue as the sky.
The child in me is as innocent as a newborn baby.
The child in me wants to be an eagle that picks his food
high up in the sky.
The child in me would like to be a fish so that I can swim in the sea.

Kaliegh Jackson (9)
Parkway Primary School, Earith

A Family Poem

My auntie likes sleeping,
She doesn't like weeping,
She crawls along the ceiling,
And she has a bad feeling.

My mum likes to shout,
She eats a lot of sprouts,
She doesn't like to walk about,
And she has loads of money in her bank account.

My older sister is a really good pincher,
She doesn't really like her teacher,
She is not a very good keeper,
And she isn't a very good sleeper.

My second older sister thinks she's so cool,
And she really likes to go to school,
She eats a lot of chicken and chips,
And she's got some big, big hips.

Anthony Esiape-Pinnock (9)
Parkway Primary School, Earith

My Family Is Just So Weird

My mum lets me play in the snow,
But it was too cold though.
My brother said, 'Get out of my room!'
So I rushed out in a zoom.
I blasted off to my sister's room,
She started shouting at me for no reason,
I wanted to put her into treason.
On that day I went to my cousin's house,
I suddenly saw a big fat mouse!

Shelly Lang (9)
Parkway Primary School, Earith

Lava

The hot bubbling lava is as hot as
The sun.
The hot bubbling lava like the
Fire's breath.
The hot bubbling lava erupts like
A madman.
The hot bubbling lava, the hot
Bubbling lava.
The hot whoosh! It destroys
The city.
The hot bubbling lava, me, I don't
Want to talk about it.

Charlie Benn (10)
Parkway Primary School, Earith

Furniture

He says to himself 'Come and sit on me,
I am a bed and I am comfy!'
He says to himself 'Put your stuff on me
I won't bite!
Just make sure that it is light!'
He says to himself 'Come and sit with me,
We can eat and watch TV!'
'Eat your breakfast, eat it fast,
For this table will not last!'
When the owner goes away . . .
The furniture will come out and play!

Peter Homewood (10)
Parkway Primary School, Earith

The Big Match

The match is underway
The home team run away
The other team is one nil up
That was a bit of luck
The keeper takes the blame
My money's down the drain

The team has a shot
The home team had a plot
They tackled them like mad
They were very bad
A couple more went in
They had a great big grin
They scored a couple more
We looked down on the floor

They scored another four
The crowd were getting bored
The game was very one-sided
The away team wouldn't of minded
At the end it was twenty to none
The home team blamed it on the sun
The winning team had a drink
The home team had to think.

Lee Bulling (10)
Parkway Primary School, Earith

Dragons

Dragons lived in Hong Kong some say
They're strong but I think they're wrong
We sing of them in song
The mighty reptile
Whose skins are old
So I'm told
They love gold
The treasure they pile.

Jahvade Francis (9)
Parkway Primary School, Earith

The Environment

Litter is wrong, we do not like it
If you see it, go and spike it
Keep it clean
Don't be mean
Don't make it a mess
Keep it clean, that's the best
The grass is green
The sky is blue
Natural beauty
Like me and you
When the incinerator begins to work
The sky will fill with smoke and dirt
The trees will die, its leaves will drop off
Then you and me will start to cough
Keep it clean, is all I ask
A lesson taught from the past
The air I need, the air I breathe
Words of wisdom, please take heed.

Victoria England (9)
Parkway Primary School, Earith

My Mum

My mum is very smelly
And she had a little belly
It will get big
She will wear a wig
She dances at the ball
She always cleans the hall
She kicks bent
She always takes scent
She is a cutie
Always looking for her boot.

Georgie Benton (9)
Parkway Primary School, Earith

Dragons

Baby dragons are small
They fit in a pool
They like to eat
Things that are sweet
They live in air
At the fair
They go on fairground rides
That are very wide!

Kirstie Gavin (10)
Parkway Primary School, Earith

Not Tidying Your Room

There was a girl
Who did not do her room
Her mum saisd 'That is not good
So do it again nicely.'
She always says 'I'm done'
Her mum always come up the
Stairs and at her daughter she
Glares and throws her down
The stairs.

Charlee Smith (10)
Parkway Primary School, Earith

The Sun

The sun is hot as it shines towards you,
It tries to grab you in its huge ball of fire.
You see his hot toes walking through
The dark blue sky,
The sun is like a hot oven on full gas mark
As it shines brightly in the sky
It looks like he smiles at you.

Rochelle Dussard (11)
Parkway Primary School, Earith

The Bet

I'll bet the home side will win,
Otherwise the money's in the bin.
After twenty minutes no one scored,
The crowd was getting bored.

At last they were 1-0 up,
That was a bit of luck.
The half-time whistle had gone,
The team talks were very long.

Someone got fouled in the area,
The man looked even scarier.
The man whose nickname is Budweiser,
Had scored the equaliser.

With ten minutes left it was getting tense,
People were watching on the fence.
The away side shot but then they missed,
'That should have went in!' the person hissed.

There was one minute left and the crowd were off their seats,
The upfronter was in the area with the goalie left to beat.
He shot the ball and through his legs,
And the ball was in the net.

The full time whistle went,
I had won the bet.
The players were cheering so loud,
That you couldn't hear half the crowd.

Ryan Bulling (10)
Parkway Primary School, Earith

Dragons

Dragons live in Hong Kong
Some people say they're strong
We sing of them in song
But I think they're wrong
The mighty reptile.
So I'm told
They love gold and
Their skins are cold
The treasure they pile.

Tony Hoang (10)
Parkway Primary School, Earith

The Football Match

I go to a football match -
And what do I see?
I see all the players -
They are looking at me!

They start the kick-off,
They kick it up high,
And what do I do?
I leap up to the sky.

They have a shot,
The crowd start to sweat,
The stadium goes quiet,
Yes! It goes in the net!

Too soon the game's over,
And we're off on our way,
But at least our team won,
So home to watch 'Match of the Day.'

Kris Boulter (10)
St John's Beaumont School, Old Windsor

The Dead Forest

In the forest a girl walked.
She saw all the rabbits.
The squirrels were climbing.
The fox was stalking.
The birds were singing.
At the roots big and thin
On the branches, twigs and leaves
On the path the beetle.

But the gang is just behind
Smoking hard!
Drop a cigarette,
The forest is alight
The gang has run!
The girl is dead.

Alexander Alderman (10)
St John's Beaumont School, Old Windsor

The New Forest

The forest is new
And the sky is blue.
The birds are tweeting,
And the squirrels are eating.
The owl has gone to sleep
And that's with the sheep.
The bees are making honey
While it's very, very sunny.
Suddenly the wolves start howling
The foxes are barking.
The animals are crowding.
They all see red and yellow flames.
The weasels stop playing games.
They all stop and stare.

Henry Taylor (10)
St John's Beaumont School, Old Windsor

The Star

Once there was a star in the sky
Who liked to make an exhibition, oh my!
He wondered why the world was so small
The people wondered when the sky would fall
The people were thinking while the star was twinkling
The people thought that the stars in space looked like their face
Yeah!
The star thought that's really, really unfair
We're unique, so smell my feet
Humans like to eat sweets
And children know all the cheats.

Jeremy Ousey (9)
St John's Beaumont School, Old Windsor

Forest's Doom

In a forest dark and gloom,
Lay the animals of its doom.
They scurry, switch and twitter
But always leave some litter.
Their homes
Are like bones,
Dirty and small.
But one stormy day, some people came,
Some dumb, the others numb.
They made a fire,
Light and bright,
So the animals ran.
But later died out into the night.

Oliver Stirling Harkin (10)
St John's Beaumont School, Old Windsor

The Creature Haunting My Dreams

For every time I go to sleep
A creature always haunts my creep
It is walking the Valley of Death
Although I try to run it runs like a beast
And it comes me by a diff side
It tries to make a feast out of me
I have no choice but to jump
When I put my hands out I hit the ground with a dunk
I wake up just as I hit, then I slowly turn my head
The figure stands beside me
With its shining green eyes waiting to strike.

Chatowa Kaluba (10)
St John's Beaumont School, Old Windsor

The Beautiful Forest

There was a beautiful forest
It was full of green trees.
The forest was peaceful
Never was there an unhappy moment
In the forest.
The sound of nature everywhere
Very calm and very peaceful
So relaxing.

Smoke and flames everywhere
Fumes and smell choking animals
Wood burning on the ground.
Dirty ash in the air.
The crackling of wood
Wildlife destroyed.

Patrick Vickery (10)
St John's Beaumont School, Old Windsor

The Fox

The fox was beautiful
With a golden gleam.
It was just like no fox
That you have ever, ever seen.
The hunters are there
They look so thrilling.
They capture the animals
Then they start killing.
They tried to capture the fox
Following its trail
But the fox was fast
So they missed its tail
The fox was hiding in the net, that was as big as me and you.
But the writing on the net said 'To Timbuktu.'

Edward Zatka-Haas (10)
St John's Beaumont School, Old Windsor

The Eagle

The eagle swooped
From its nest, into the air
Up it soars and loops
In the sky. Its eyes sharp and
Fierce, staring at the ground, looking
For its prey, it sights
A rabbit and up it goes
And circles round and round.
Down it swoops slowly
Ready for a chase
It glides back to the
Sky. Then suddenly shoots
Back, talons ready,
And snatches it up.

Ben Hollins (9)
St John's Beaumont School, Old Windsor

The Forest Fire

There was a forest a beautiful, peaceful one
With lots of animals playing in the sun.
The rabbits with their cute, furry ears
The eagles which the rabbits fear
The giraffes with their long necks
The elephants who look like they have specks
And also lots of trees
Within the trees, are the smaller animals, the fleas
But suddenly a huge fire raced towards the forest
It burned the trees down and flames came from the animals homes
The flames destroyed everything in its path
The fire had destroyed everything
The animals can never play again
Never again will the forest be a peaceful one.

Shiva Chauhan (10)
St John's Beaumont School, Old Windsor

The Firework

It was one firework night this poem does begin.
The fireworks were all beautiful they lit up red and green.
I even do remember a man drinking gin.
Then, I do remember, he tried to eat a little bean.
Then they put me on a plank of wood.
I didn't like it there.
But when I shot up in the air it felt very good.
Then my sparks went here and there,
All my sparks went everywhere.

Then suddenly I do recall
I very slowly started to fall.
And I hit a tree and not the ground.
And suddenly
I slowly found I did not hit the tree.
I hit the ground.

Jason Higgins (9)
St John's Beaumont School, Old Windsor

The Amazing Reef

In the beautiful sea the great reef was alive,
With so many fish that could swim and dive.
The fish were any colour you could name,
That's how the reef earned its fame.
So many different creatures were there,
You wouldn't know who was who and who was where
They were so happy all around,
There was not one unhappy creature to be found.

But then they came.
Huge monsters came who heard about the reef's fame.
They had tanks and suits,
As well as strange colourful boots.
The peace was broken,
And the evil fish were awoken.

Benjamin Fernando (10)
St John's Beaumont School, Old Windsor

My Family

James
My brother makes me laugh
I find it hard to stop
Yet he is a super joker
Friend, companion, helper
My brother.

Katy
Very funny
Swimming, sporty, TV,
Love her, miss her,
My sister.

Mum and Dad
They love me, they help me
Always there,
Parents.

Christopher Heywood (9)
St John's Beaumont School, Old Windsor

Dolphin

Dolphin, dolphin as you prance,
Upon the waves you dance,
People see and gasp with glee,
Water sprays as you go higher and higher.

As you swim through the waves,
All your friends make you bright,
Jumping from wave to wave,
See the sunlight in your eyes,
Then come down to the waters light.

Others spring out the blue,
People want to play with you,
Travellers hear you squeak with joy.
The sea is calm
The sea is warm
Just the way you like it to be.

Stephanie Brooks (10)
St Katherine's CP School, Snodland

Flowers

Flowers grow very slow
Then blossom very well
Then they start to show
Their colours they
Tighten up like a
Rainbow shows.
Then comes the
Winter and kills
All the flowers.
Here comes summer
Away goes all the
Rain, and flowers
Grow again.

Jessica Randall (9)
St Katherine's CP School, Snodland

Time For Autumn

The frosty crackled leaves ready for autumn,
The bare trees with no leaves.
The wind wildly blowing through the air.
But no one shouting here and there.

All the trees look like they're dead,
But from this day they still will grow,
With new leaves all bright you never know.

I hope the trees will ever grow,
For the crows that live,
So autumn always come never go
For to make the leaves flowing on the ground.

Charlotte Punyer (10)
St Katherine's CP School, Snodland

The Dancing Stallion

Its ballet-type legs prance on the grass
It holds its head high as it comes past
Its pricked up ears are as soft as snow
But this horse is gentle, do you know.

It dances all day
It dances all night
But this clever creature is a wonderful sight.

It'll dance in circles
It'll dance in squares
Stop it dancing
You won't dare!

Rebecca Merry (10)
St Katherine's CP School, Snodland

My Crazy Dog

My pet dog she is Rosie and she's so fluffy
She's the fluffiest dog I know.
She's half rat but acts like one
So I can't even think of blaming you.

She's so noisy she's louder than a sobbing baby
So get me out of here
She's getting on my nerves
So help me out of this.

Rosie is really mad because
She's faster than a cheetah that is really mad
She crawls over my head, I'm getting boiling mad
But I can't moan because I have to live with her.

I could say more and more but that's enough.

George Cooke (10)
St Katherine's CP School, Snodland

Seasons

Summer is the best,
Because of the tropical sun,
Always glowing in the sky.
Autumn has mighty winds,
That hurries like a race,
And sprinkles leaves to the ground.
Spring is the one with lots of flowers,
Like poppies, tulips and more,
And newborn animals too.
Lastly there is winter,
That is the most fun season of them all,
Especially when making snowmen.
I like seasons they're the greatest.

Natalie Bush (10)
St Katherine's CP School, Snodland

My Doggie Annie

Annie
Is a bit dumb,
She can be stupid,
She can be fun.

Annie
She acts like she's two,
But she really is fine,
She chases flies around the garden,
Runs around the house.

Annie
Rests at night,
Plays all day,
And never gives up, always wants to play.

Annie
Although she is dumb,
She still is fun,
Oh, and one little thing,
She eats from a bin.

Charlotte Phillips (9)
St Katherine's CP School, Snodland

Mable My Dog

Mable my dog loves to run about.
Mable my dog loves to fight with my mum and I.
Mable my dog perches by the radiator peacefully.
Mable my dog loves to play with her squeaker.
Mable my dog loves to leap around with a sprinkler.
Mable my dog is as white as a cloud.
Mable my dog has a dirty paw.
Mable my dog has a mouth with dirty fur.

Alice White (9)
St Katherine's CP School, Snodland

Animals

I like kittens and I like cats
I like snakes and I like rats
I like monkeys swinging through the trees
But the one thing I hate is buzzing bees.

I like rabbits and I like dogs
I like horses and I like frogs
I also like hopping fleas
But the one thing I hate is buzzing bees.

I like dolphins and I like snails
I like sparrows and I like whales
I like magpies in the trees
But the one thing I hate is buzzing bees.

I like hamsters and I like cows
I like spiders and I like owls
I have a question especially for you
Do you like animals? Because I do!

Megan Payne (9)
St Katherine's CP School, Snodland

The Puppy

The cuddly puppy
Like a rolling log
Like a walking robot
As a walking person
As a small rock
Like a small cushion
I love the puppy
Soft and sweet
Running in the garden
Plays with his ball
Long wavy ears
And a waggly tail too.

Ashley Randall (9)
St Katherine's CP School, Snodland

Wigit The Horse

Wigit the horse
Is a happy playful horse
Wigit the horse
Is a grey young horse
Wigit the horse
Is a very small horse
Wigit the horse
Is a soft cuddly horse
Wigit the horse
Sometimes can be rough
Wigit the horse
Loves to death the fresh juicy grass
Wigit the horse
Loves to gallop in the field full of flowers
Wigit the horse
Is an extremely kind horse
But most of all Wigit loves the other horses around him!

Charlotte Huston (9)
St Katherine's CP School, Snodland

A Monkey

As smooth as a kitten
As playful as a puppy,
As noisy as a parrot, but
As fast as a cheetah.

As friendly as a person
It can swing from its tail
It jumps like a kangaroo high in the trees
As brown as the tree it climbs.

Lindsey Gwilliam (10)
St Katherine's CP School, Snodland

Animals Under The Sea

Animals who live under the sea,
Turtles, the calmest creature in the sea
With its great big shell on its huge back
Oh what a wonderful creature.

Dolphins the most admirable creature in the sea
Their gentle totty noise,
Oh what a wonderful creature.

Starfish, the noiseless creatures in the sea and the slickest,
Oh what a wonderful creature.

Fiercest creature in the sea
The terrible gruesome creature, this is the shark!
Oh what a scary creature.

Well, all these wonderful creatures
I could go on forever.

Laura Turner (9)
St Katherine's CP School, Snodland

The Weather

Rainbows are colours in the sky
Bright and beautiful and up so high
In my dreams I fly and soar
Above, the birds squeal and caw
In the distance the trees are wet
Snowy weather is coming, that I'll bet
As the snow fell on the ground
It hardly makes any sound
The wind was cold as it blew
It was freezing out, that I knew
I put on my coat, my scarf, my hat
I wrapped up warm, my boots on the mat
I opened the door and ran down the path
I met all my friends and we had such a laugh.

Lauren Baker (10)
St Katherine's CP School, Snodland

Dolphin

Dolphin, dolphin up you rise
Do your thing and it will make you wise
From the water blue and glistening
People gaze from all around
Water sprays as you spring
From the glittering, warm, blue sea.

Your beautiful coat shines in the sun
As you swim from wave to wave
Then you jump as high as you can
So people gasp at the sight
Then you land back in the sea
And meet your friends at the bottom of the seabed.

You squeak with bliss
As you jump inch by inch
You play with your friends
And you play with the waves
The sea is warm
The sea is calm.

Rachel Andrews (9)
St Katherine's CP School, Snodland

Above And Below

I'm in my flat
Cars below me
Tall ones, short ones, thin ones, fat ones,
Even multicoloured ones.

I'm in my flat
Voices below me
Loud ones, quiet ones, big ones, small ones,
Even foreign ones.

I'm in my flat
Aeroplanes above me
Noisy ones, silent ones, fast ones, slow ones,
Even paper ones.

Sam Shaw (9)
St Katherine's CP School, Snodland

My Cat

My cat is called Toots, he's as black as night
He's amazingly smart, he can play darts.
He plays with his tail as any cat would.
He's loving and calm
But with a streak of lightning he's hiding for cover.

He has an elegant figure
With two glazing, luminous green eyes
And two pricked up ears and
A swishing, furry tail.

My cat's a super cat
It can fly through the sky like a hawk in pursuit of a feeble
scurrying mouse.
He can sprint on its four sturdy legs as fast as sound.

Sam Robinson (10)
St Katherine's CP School, Snodland

Different Animals

Frogs
Frogs are all different
Colours, some red, some green
I have not seen them all
Because there are all too many.
They creep the town, like terrorists
From the city with
Bloodsucking eyes which can
Kill you with sacredness.

Birds
Birds can fly like an army jet plane
They flap their wings like elephants
Shaking their ears when they are drenched to the skin.
Birds have beaks and triple-coloured feathers
Which can make the birds fly to places which
Humans have never seen before.

Ryan Williams (9)
St Katherine's CP School, Snodland

A Kitten's Adventures

A soft kitten scurries off to play.

Little licks lash across her body while she gets cleaned
by her mother.
Imaginative mind holds the kitten back from working and relaxing.
Tiger-like impressions make the soft kitten get bored of her dad.
Trying to pounce on a fly her mother lets her go and play outside.
Loud pants off the dog make the kitten scared so she throws
a ball at him.
Elly runs chasing after the kitten and jumps for the ball
but rolls away.

Kicking and scratching she climbed down a hole where she
met a rabbit.
Intently scared the rabbit shows the kitten the way out.
Trying hard to push herself and she gets tired.
Tired out she tries going to sleep.
Eventually she falls asleep.
Now dozing she purrs peacefully.

Kirsty Brooker (9)
St Katherine's CP School, Snodland

Duelling Dragons

Duelling dragons.
Twisting and turning in the night's sky.
Fire dragon
Fierce with piercing black eyes,
Scales bright red.
Ice dragon,
Cool and sleek, eyes crisp and clear,
Scales white.
Both ferocious,
With gripping claws and swinging tails,
Teeth sharp, fire hot from their jaws.
Who will dominate the night skies?
Only morning will tell.

Jessica Archer (10)
St Katherine's CP School, Snodland

The Countryside

The sun is blazing,
To show wondrous blossom trees,
The old, large oak is the centre of it all,
Squirrels running freely,
Scampering about,
A field mouse's head poking out of the hay,
The horses galloping around are so tall and proud,
While the little hare scampers around all day.

The night is full of noise,
For the badger and the fox,
Are on the prowl for their meal,
It may be field mice or a little shrew,
But beyond in the stream,
The frogs sit on the bank,
They start croaking as loud as they can.

At sunrise the proud cockerel,
Stands on the gate and crows,
The squirrels peek out of the trunk of the old, oak
Its branches raised like arms,
The trunk of the tree is so thick and strong,
The branches alone are rough and wide,
The bright, red poppies surround it.

Georgia Smith (10)
St Katherine's CP School, Snodland

My Dog

My dog likes to fetch when I throw him a ball
He brings it back when I call
My dog likes to have a swim
He has to get out when the light gets dim
When it's morning we fill it deep
And in the evening he goes to sleep.

Samantha Berry (10)
St Katherine's CP School, Snodland

King Henry VIII

King Henry was as big as a boar,
He ate so much he always wanted more.
King Henry was fond of cockfighting,
He even built his own pit.
Any cocks that died were put on a spit,
He spent all his money on food, women and wine.
But it still didn't make him happy because he was miserable
                                        most of the time.
King Henry had six wives, one died, one survived.
Two were beheaded, two divorced.
One divorced because she looked like a horse.
King Henry fathered three surviving children, two girls and a boy.
It was only the boy who brought him joy.
King Henry died in 1547 aged fifty-six.
No one was sorry to see him go.
His son Edward V was then made king.
But that's another story.
Now I must go.

Declan McMorrow (10)
St Katherine's CP School, Snodland

Animals

The animals in the world,
Elephants - with their noisy trunk,
Tigers - with their fierce teeth,
Dogs - with their floppy ears,
Cats - with their fluffy tails,
Dolphins - with their strong bodies,
Cheetahs - with their fast legs,
I could go on forever . . .

Charlotte Bungay (9)
St Katherine's CP School, Snodland

Summer Times

In the summer it's very hot,
How do babies sleep in their cot?
All the flowers are so bright,
They're such a wonderful sight.
Lots of people go out to play,
Whereas parents have big water bills to pay.
Not many people stay inside,
Lots of people go down to the seaside.
People down at the beach eating ice cream,
They thought it was a dream.
Teenagers don't go in the pool,
Because they think it's not cool.
All the people have so much fun,
Playing in the sun.
Children try to row their boat,
Going round and round a castle moat.
All the children play with water guns,
In the beaming sun.
Summer now fades away,
Ahead of us now, the cold blue winter days.

Declan O'Connell (10)
St Katherine's CP School, Snodland

A Frog

As bouncy as a trampoline
It eats flies
Its got a long tongue
As green as someone being sick
As light as a feather
It has four legs
It jumps from one place to another.

Geoffrey Robinson (10)
St Katherine's CP School, Snodland

My Pets

I have twenty-one pets in all,
Thirteen birds, two dogs, two mice, one lizard, one rat, one cat
and a snake.
They're all lovely to have,
But not when it comes to cleaning them out.

I have four quails,
Their names are Dumbledore, Harry, Malfoy and Hagrid.
They're all pleasant to have,
But they make such a racket.

I have four zebra finches,
Their names are Sam and Ella, Stanley and Casper.
They're lovely to have,
But they lay too many eggs.

I have a golden song sparrow,
His name is Cheese.
He's delightful to have,
But he's extremely shy.

I have a red-eared waxbill,
His name is Ane.
He's nice to have,
But he's really quick.

I have an albino budgie,
His name is Snowball.
He's great to have,
But he always makes a mess.

I have an orange canary,
His name is Tango.
He's fabulous to have,
But he lets others push him around.

I have a cockatiel,
Her name is Zoe.
She's brilliant to have,
But she chewed through her ladder.

I have two dogs,
Their names are Ollie and Tye.
They're excellent to have,
But they chew everything up.

I have two mice and a rat,
Their names are Salt, Pepper and Charlie.
They're splendid to have,
But they might bite.

I have a cat
Her name is Mittens.
She's fantastic to have,
But I hardly ever see her.

I have a snake and a lizard,
Their names are Jake and Slinky.
They're super to have,
But they eat mice and maggots.

I love all my pets,
Except for one or two problems.

Natasha Manning (9)
St Katherine's CP School, Snodland

The Horse

The cuddly horse,
Soft, cute,
Like a special tiger bear teddy,
Like a special diamond that you look at every day,
It runs along the field like a small dog,
Like a fluffy kitten
As gentle as a newborn baby,
As soft as a cuddly teddy bear,
I love my horse he is the best.

Rose-Jane King (9)
St Katherine's CP School, Snodland

Pigs

My mum likes pigs, I don't know why
They're pink and smelly and live in a sty,
They grunt and squeal for most of the day,
And other times they roll in the hay.

They scream and shout when food's about,
They seek it out with their snouts,
They push and shove to get their fill,
And it's all thanks to Farmer Bill!

They laze about in the sun,
There's no work to be done,
Sometimes they get up for a drink,
But, oh my God do they stink!

They're fattened up, the little porkers,
Some are even burned into corkers,
Into the pan . . . let's not be too hasty,
Perhaps that's why she likes them . . . they're so tasty!

Chloe Johnstone (11)
St Katherine's CP School, Snodland

The Newborn Baby Cousin

As cute as a newborn baby,
Soft, cuddly
Like a lovely, snuggled up baby asleep,
As small as a baby kitten,
As cute as her mum and dad,
I love my baby cousin Victoria,
Like a dark silent night,
She crawls around the floor.

Sophie Ellis (9)
St Katherine's CP School, Snodland

Was I Dreaming?

What is that noise down in the garden?
It might be the dog, whining, crying,
I'll take a look, I go downstairs,
The worst I can see are grizzly bears.

I walk through the living room, dining room, kitchen,
On outside, into the garden,
I'm gobsmached, afraid, I can't even speak,
I'm so scared, I look down at my feet.

The whole world has changed and turned into a forest,
The kennel, the playhouse have turned into trees,
I move on, I walk, on into the darkness,
I hear a noise, I scuttle behind a tree.

A shadow appears, it comes closer and closer,
I feel breath on my neck, the tension is building,
I close my eyes, someone calls my name,
My mum's standing next to the house, no more trees in sight.,

Christopher Carr (10)
St Katherine's CP School, Snodland

The Rainbow

Rain, rain pouring down, splish, splash on the ground,
When it stops we shout, hooray!
Then the sun comes out to play,
We look into the sky above,
And see a beautiful coloured arch,
All the colours that we can see,
Make up a rainbow as pretty as can be.

Laura Roope (11)
St Katherine's CP School, Snodland

All About Everything

The ocean roars
Like the wild boars
Seas will crash
And waves will smash

Trees will rustle
Creatures will bustle
Lions will roar
While the sloth will snore

Cheetahs run
But I am still not done
Sharks will swim
While servants bow to whim

While our planet lies
Many things die
While our planet spins
No one wins

While dogs will bark
The teachers mark
As guns fire
Cleaners have their hire
Darkness is nigh
It's time to say goodbye.

Jordan Penney (10)
St Katherine's CP School, Snodland

The Busy City - Haiku

A busy city
People rushing all around
Cars are all around.

Ryan Fuller (9)
St Katherine's CP School, Snodland

Oh Homework!

Oh homework!
I wish I could wash you
Down the drain
And never see you again.
Homework!
You're giving me a pain.

I'd rather swim
With a man-eating shark,
Then work out my English with you.
Homework! Oh homework!
You're giving me fits.

Homework! Homework!
You're a bit of a bore,
And also you become a chore!
Oh homework!
I hate you!

Matthew Punyer (11)
St Katherine's CP School, Snodland

Autumn

Autumn is very breezy
The leaves spiral onto the ground
Leaves all around
Crunching like cornflakes.

Trees losing their leaves
Birds burying themselves in their nests
Children jumping in piles of leaves
Leaves flying everywhere.

Samantha Stevens (9)
St Katherine's CP School, Snodland

Sports

Sports are fun games
But only when they're played right
Especially football duels
No beating
No cheating
Tennis is also fun
No rabbling
Or no scrabbling
All but Britain wins trophy
Henman never wins a match
While Rusdeski's on the run
Roddick winning Wimbledon
Cricket is a great game
Innings, outs and misses
All these things you need
For playing the game
And having fame.

Tom Jarmyn (10)
St Katherine's CP School, Snodland

The Nightmare

Monsters walk around at night
Blacker than night
In your sight
Never bright.

Ghosts in a graveyard
Cannot be heard
Banging hard against the floor
Open the door
Ah! Ah! Ah!

Matthew Cradduck (11)
St Katherine's CP School, Snodland

Michael Poem

This week for my homework
I was asked to write a poem.
So I had to think of what to write
And decided to write about Michael Owen.

He's quick when he's got the ball
And when he hasn't he still moves fast.
He does little runs all over the pitch
He twists and turns on the grass.

And when he gets the ball
He can shoot from any place.
The ball moves with such power as it
Bounces off his boot.

The ball shoots into the top corner
And smashes into the back of the net.
If you need to score a goal
Michael Owen's your best bet.

Ethan Martin (11)
St Katherine's CP School, Snodland

Snow

Flurries of snow falling down to the ground
Making no sound
Swirling round and round
People making snowmen on the ground
Snow in the trees
But there's no bees
Clear blue skies
Children's faces filled with surprise
At the sunrise
Children playing on the slides
Birds glide through snow painted sky
Time to say goodbye.

Rebecca Field (11)
St Katherine's CP School, Snodland

Snow

Glistening, glowing, sparkling, it's snowing
Cold and white, it snowed through the night
Soft on the ground, there's snow all around
Everyone slipping, everyone sliding,
Everyone skating everyone gliding.
The children outside they sing and they play,
They run and hide through night and through day.
Whilst people do sleep the snow falls right down,
It covers the ground like a white dressing gown.
The birds outside stand cold as ice
But the people inside are cosy and nice.
The creatures all hide in their nests, in their hives.
The wind blows so bitter it's the middle of winter.
The world was all covered in a white blanket
Believe me it's true, it was a marvellous sight for me and for you.

Nicola Paget (10)
St Katherine's CP School, Snodland

The Banger

The banger,
Shiny, battered,
Like a stop car,
Like a noisy engine,
It races round the track,
Like a jump jet,
As quick as a cheetah,
As noisy as a dragon,
I like the banger.

Keith Jenner (10)
St Katherine's CP School, Snodland

Pandora's Box

'Is there a catch, let's try the latch!'
Fear, death, and diseases escape,
Travel the land, the landscapes,
Darkness creeps, hides under the stairs,
Disease sneaks under the apples and pears,
Death kills millions of people in swarms,
The dead's loved ones cry and moan,
Screaming, crying, moaning, dying,
Pandora has opened the box,
'Is there a catch, let's try the latch!'
People shouting, eyes sore,
This will last for evermore,
Pandora shuts the box, and then,
She hears a voice from within,
'Help, help' a voice shouts.
'It is Hope, let me out!'
Pandora opens the box once more,
Out flies something, she stares in
Pandora has opened the box
'Is there a catch let's try the latch!'
'It is Hope, I come to save you from
The evil deeds you've called to come.'
Hope flutters about making it peaceful once more
But in its heart, the very core,
Pandora has opened the box,
There is no putting this back,
Pretty girl but brains you lack,
But all in all despite pretty locks
Pandora opened the box!

Chloe Manning (11)
St Katherine's CP School, Snodland

When I Fish

The water was glistening in the sun.
The pike were swimming fast and having fun.
Ducks are big and some are small.
Some ducks are even very tall.

We sit and wait for a bite
Hoping to catch a fish in the light.
When you get a bite
You strike hoping it's a pike.

You have to be quick and reel it in.
Carefully, watch out for their sharp fin.
Cast the net, pull it in and lift it up.
Unhook the fish and have a look
And write it in your book.
Make a wish and say goodbye to the fish.

Daniel Crosby (9)
St Katherine's CP School, Snodland

Reunions

There was an international phone call
Out of the blue
I sat and wondered who.

A friend I had not seen for so long
Would we remember things from the past?
Or would we have long awkward moments that last.

The doorbell rings
And friends have arrived
Laughter and jokes
Memories survived
No awkward moments dragging past
Just a friendship that will last and last.

Aisling Gilham (11)
St Katherine's CP School, Snodland

The Fishing Trip

As I pack up my fishing gear
I start to get very excited.
I start to imagine what type of fish we might catch
And daydream about how many.

At last we arrive at the fishing lake
I see the trees and bushes swaying.
I stand and watch the ripples on the water
And see air bubbles popping on the surface.

I cast out for the first time, my weight soon bobbed under the water.
Soon I was towing a good-sized fish through the water.
I couldn't believe my luck,
After a short time I was standing on the bank
Having my picture taken with a carp.

After our picnic lunch and a few more catches,
Dad and I pack up our fishing gear, this takes quite a while.
One last walk around the lake, one last look.
We pack up the van and head for home, I can't wait to tell everyone.

Reece Allen (10)
St Katherine's CP School, Snodland

Fairy Kingdom

In a fairy kingdom
Lies a fairy town
Fairies flying upwards
Fairies flying down
Fairies flying side to side
Granting all the wishes
Fairies trying very hard
To do their little deeds
Fairies flying back to home
Curling up in bed
As they turn out all the lights
'Goodnight' the littlest said.

Catharine Laverty (11)
St Katherine's CP School, Snodland

The Cat

My cat is very fat.
She likes my big hat.
If my cat sees a rat she flies like a bat.
And by the way my cat is very fat.

She sits on her tail but don't fetch the mail.
Because she's not a dog but a big fat cat.
Because she's so fat she sits on a hat.
The fat cat that sits on the mat.

Aaron Baxter (10)
St Katherine's CP School, Snodland

My Mum

As lovely as can be,
As beautiful as a butterfly,
As friendly as a puppy bought from the shop,
As fast as a tiger from the zoo,
As good as a dad,
As big as a tree in the garden,
As brave as a boy,
As swift as the stars,
Always there for me.

Michael Stevens (10)
St Katherine's CP School, Snodland

Fishes

Fishes swish their tails, fishes go pop, pop, pop
Fishes use their fins for when they swim
Fishes swim across the sea jumping in the summer sky
Fishes dive into the clear blue sea.

Katie Filmer (7)
St Katherine's CP School, Snodland

Ten Little Starfish

Ten little starfish lying in the light blue sea,
Then one was gone then there were nine.
Nine little starfish lying in the light blue sea,
Then one was gone then there were eight.
Eight little starfish lying in the light blue sea,
Then one was gone then there were seven.
Seven little starfish lying in the light blue sea,
Then one was gone then there were six.

Lauren Ivy (7)
St Katherine's CP School, Snodland

Ghost Train

As fast as a cheetah
As scary as the dark
Like a nightmare at night
As ghostly as the moon
It's tempting to go on but I don't want to lose my mum
As dark as the colour black
Like a monster creeping
I get on it and I am gone.

Katy Morgan (10)
St Katherine's CP School, Snodland

Eagle

As gold as treasure
It swoops like a kite in the sky
Faster than a racing car
This predator is evil when he claws his prey
Talons as sharp as knives
Feathers as shiny as the sun
Beak like a hook
Beautiful patterns on his wings on his back.

Alex Scott (11)
St Katherine's CP School, Snodland

Ten Little Fairies

Ten little fairies standing in a line
One broke its leg and then there were nine.
Nine little fairies looking through a gate
One banged her head and then there were eight.
Eight little fairies going to Devon
One went the wrong way and then there were seven.
Seven little fairies picking up a stick
One got a splinter and then there were six.
Six little fairies going for a dive
One was drowning and then there were five.
Five little fairies standing on the floor
One was flying and then there were four.
Four little fairies looking up a tree
One looked down and then there were three.
Three little fairies sitting in a show
One was looking for a wing and then there were two.
Two little fairies standing on a drum
One lost her shoe and then there was one.

Hannah Morgan (7)
St Katherine's CP School, Snodland

Eleven Little Pigs

Eleven little pigs got eaten by a hen then there were ten.
Ten little pigs standing in a vine, one fell over then there were nine.
Nine little pigs fall over then there were eight.
Eight little pigs went to Devon, one got lost then there were seven.
Seven little pigs went to fix a car then there were six.
Six little pigs went to a hive, then there were five.
Five little pigs went to get more, one got lost then there were four.
Four little pigs went to a bee then there were three.
Three little pigs went to the zoo then there were two.
Two little pigs weighed a ton, then there was one.

Ben Kember (8)
St Katherine's CP School, Snodland

Ten Little Puppies

Ten little puppies playing in a line
One fell over then there were nine
Nine little puppies play on the light
One went off then there were eight
Eight little puppies, one went to Devon
One got left behind then there were seven
Seven little puppies, one ate Weetabix
One went to bed then there were six
Six little puppies, one dived
One went swimming then there were five
Five little puppies running around, one hurt its paw
And went and played then there were four
Four little puppies jumping, banged in a tree
One went asleep then there were three
Three little puppies ate stew
One went to play then there were two
Two little puppies had a race, one won
One lost, then there was one.

Leanne Tattersall (8)
St Katherine's CP School, Snodland

Fast Food

Rainbow trout
Brussels sprouts
Home-made
Lemonade
Spicy dips
Orange pips
Boiled ham
Gooey jam
T-bone steak
Get a milkshake
Chocolate flake
Fairy cake.

Matthew Whitewood (8)
St Katherine's CP School, Snodland

Come And Eat

Chips and hake, strawberry milkshake
Come and eat! Come and eat!
My ice, chicken spice
Come and eat! Come and eat!
Chocolate cream, like a stream.
Come and eat! Come and eat!
Chocolate flake, like a bucket of snakes
Come and eat! Come and eat!
Boiled ham, roasted lamb.
Come and eat! Come and eat!
Chocolate flake, fairy cake.
Come and eat! Come and eat!
Fish and chips, spicy dips.
Come and eat! Come and eat!

Sheri Matthews (7)
St Katherine's CP School, Snodland

Anger

The colour of anger is red like a blaze.
It tastes like orange chillies bubbling.
That's anger!
It smells like a boiling fire choking you.
It looks like a steaming kettle whistling.
That's anger!
It sounds like a train screeching to a halt.
It feels like being scalded by hot tea.
That's anger!

Georgia-Rose Burt (9)
St Katherine's CP School, Snodland

Sad

Sad is blue like the rain on a rainy day.
Sad tastes like a lone drop of water.
Sad smells like the blue lonely sky.
Sad looks like wet tears.
Sad sounds like someone crying.
Sad feels like a friendless person.

Ryan Summers Parker (9)
St Katherine's CP School, Snodland

Fear

Fear is black like the middle of space
Fear tastes like black pears
Fear smells like lava
Fear looks like a foggy storm
Fear sounds like a screeching car
Fear feels like being dead.

Joe Ward (8)
St Katherine's CP School, Snodland

Love

Love is the colour of red roses
Love tastes like pink raspberries
Love is the smell of freshly cut daisies
Love looks like bright lipstick
Love sounds like a girl laughing
Love feels like my heart going boom, boom, boom.

Sapphire Barnes (9)
St Katherine's CP School, Snodland

Happiness

Happiness is yellow like a lovely cloud not making a sound.
It tastes like a juicy lemon.
It smells like a sour flower.
It looks like children playing quietly saying all different words.
It sounds like a singing bird
It feels like a cat rubbing against my legs.

Lucy Scoble (9)
St Katherine's CP School, Snodland

Fear

Fear is like black storms
Fear tastes like cold rice pudding
Fear smells like wet tarmac
Fear looks like a night-time street
Fear sounds like hailstones dropping on the path
Fear feels like you've got butterflies in your tummy.

Mitchel Worsley (8)
St Katherine's CP School, Snodland

Fear

Fear is black like a storm coming from the night sky.
It tastes like cold mouldy pudding that is in front of you.
Fear smells like soggy dirt outside in your garden.
It looks like night when it's raining.
Fear sounds like ghosts in the sky.
It feels like being alone.

Sam Head (9)
St Katherine's CP School, Snodland

Fear

Fear is black like falling down a dark ditch.
Fear tastes like poisoned apple.
Fear smells like burned curtains.
Fear looks dark like a lightless cave.
Fear sounds like rustling bushes.
Fear feels like you are alone but you think there is someone
behind you.

Francesca Chambers (9)
St Katherine's CP School, Snodland

Fear

Fear is like a black stormy cloud.
Fear tastes like a mouldy apple.
Fear smells like a dripping cellar.
Fear sounds like a rat crawling in the sewage.
Fear feels like being punched down the hole.
Fear looks like a hunted house.

Aaron Salisbury (9)
St Katherine's CP School, Snodland

Excited

Excited is loads of bright colours,
Excited tastes like chocolate and doughnuts,
Excited smells like delicious sweets,
Excited looks like a wild adventure,
Excited sounds like children laughing,
Excited makes me feel like a dancing rocket about to explode,
Excited makes you want to join in.

Liane Twomlow (9)
St Katherine's CP School, Snodland

Fright

Fright is black like a lonesome street.
Fright tastes like vampire blood dripping from the mouth.
Fright smells like cold cabbage from a ditch.
Fright looks like a mummy crossing the road.
Fright sounds like Dracula biting you.
Fright feels like a shiver up your spine.

Ellie Ryell (8)
St Katherine's CP School, Snodland

Excitement

Excitement is like a juicy orange.
It tastes like delicious chocolate and sweets.
It smells like freshly cut flowers.
It looks like colourful bright fireworks.
It sounds like newly found languages.
It feels like you're uncontrollable and you can never sleep.

Jordan Lord (9)
St Katherine's CP School, Snodland

Fear

Fear is as black as space.
Fear tastes like rotten apples.
Fear smells like the sewage works.
Fear sounds like the noisiest street in the world.
Fear feels like being punched down a hole.

Leon Desbruslais (8)
St Katherine's CP School, Snodland

Love

Love is red like a fine day.
Love tastes like a sweet strawberry.
Love looks like the sun going down.
Love smells like fresh candyfloss.
Love sounds like birds singing in the trees.

Lois Beecroft (9)
St Katherine's CP School, Snodland

The Week

Monday we first start the school
Tuesday I stay by the rules
Wednesday we knocked our heads on the walls
Thursday it was all nice and cool
Friday we go to the gym in the hall
Saturday I like to go to the mall
Sunday I sit back and stay in bed all day.

Bethany Sterrett (8)
St Katherine's CP School, Snodland

Love

Love is the colour of a pink heart beaming like mad.
Love tastes like juicy apples wanting to be eaten.
Love smells like some lovely strawberries hanging from a tree.
Love sounds like a rose waiting to be picked.
Love feels like smooth skin wanting to be stroked.
Love looks like a couple kissing.

Ashlea Baker (8)
St Katherine's CP School, Snodland

Fear

Fear is like black clouds in the moonlight sky,
That's fear.
It tastes like hot burnt toast,
It smells musty, damp and wet like someone just cried,
That's fear.
It looks like a fire when it's all smoky,
It sounds like wind rushing in the moonlight sky,
That's fear.
It feels like rain dripping down on you
And it feels like it's near and you are lonely.
That's fear.

Emma Marchant (9)
St Katherine's CP School, Snodland

Love

Love is pink as a tremendously juicy jelly baby,
Love tastes like a ripe box of strawberries,
Love smells like a crispy, creamy, flaky galaxy,
Love looks like a blooming red rose,
Love sounds like a mad thumping heart beating to the music,
Love feels like a dreamy dream.

Jessica Goodhew (8)
St Katherine's CP School, Snodland

Love

Love is sweet like real juicy strawberries
It tastes like biting into a brand new green, shiny, juicy apple
It smells like freshly grown roses in a field
It looks like a country woodland with the sun glaring on you
It sounds like a twittering bird in the morning
It feels like a kitten rubbing its fluffy hair on your leg.

Daniel Hobbs (9)
St Katherine's CP School, Snodland

The Big Blue Whale

The size of a playground
It moves slowly around and around
Opens his mouth to gulp
When he uses his pulse
You never realise how big and monstrous
Until you see the real thing
And then you want to give it a wedding ring
Deep, deep it goes through the water
And then through Malta.

Patrick Woolley (10)
St Katherine's CP School, Snodland

The Cat - Haiku

Looking at a rat
With fur as black as darkness
Tasty prey for tea.

Hannah Cheesewright (9)
St Katherine's CP School, Snodland

Snowy Days

The snow is like a white blanket on the floor
It looks like candyfloss on your door
The snow looks like flowers growing
It's really just the whole world snowing
In the night it snows so hard
It covers your entire backyard!
When the snow is wild
It could wake a little child
In the morning when it's light
You can have a snowball fight.

Kerryann Reynolds (10)
St Katherine's CP School, Snodland

The Sun

The sun is a sparkly orange buoy floating in outer space
The sun is a pound coin thrown up in the air
The sun is a golden pen
The sun is an orange car
The sun is a sparkling gel pen leaving a glitter trail
The sun is a giant's wig
The sun is a shiny plate
The sun is a lightning bolt.

James Randall (10)
St Katherine's CP School, Snodland

The Snow - Haiku

Snow falling softly
Snow falling makes a blanket
And then disappears.

Nicky Schooling (10)
St Katherine's CP School, Snodland

Best Friend

Jack is my best friend,
We play together in school.
He's tall and blonde and clever,
And when he dances he is cool.

Jack is my best friend,
He lets me go round his house.
He is as loud as a lion,
I'm small like a mouse!

Lewis Nyberg (10)
St Katherine's CP School, Snodland

The World

Trees are dark green now.
Flowers shining all the time.
The sky is so blue.
Bushes are so prickly.
People always like the sun.

Lucy Jones (9)
St Katherine's CP School, Snodland

Snow

Snow is exciting, lovely
Run and you can hear birds singing and children laughing
Snow is like a shining white, polar bear diving in an icy pool
Snow if it lived would be an eagle diving down for its prey
Snow is like Miss Wilson throwing a piece of paper in the bin
Snow is like wool falling from a sheared sheep onto the ground.

Thomas Webley (10)
St Katherine's CP School, Snodland

Birds

Birds are now eating
Birds are beginning sleeping
Birds are now waking
Birds start playing
Birds are having fun with friends
The birds are now gone.

Rachael Pett (9)
St Katherine's CP School, Snodland

My Cat Snowy

My cat Snowy is as fluffy as a cotton wool ball
He likes walking briskly on the frozen swimming pool.
My cat Snowy is as fast as a flash of light
He likes wandering around in the starry night.
My cat Snowy is as warm as a red fire
But he is a bit of a selfish liar.
My cat Snowy is as cute as a fluffy teddy bear
Adores sniffing the clean, fresh air.
My cat Snowy at the end of the day
Is a loving caring cat who likes lying on hay.

Ellie Thomas (9)
St Katherine's CP School, Snodland

Birds

Birds fly in the air
They just land on twigs as well
They flap their wings
When they're flying in the air
I saw one little one dead.

Matthew Wade (10)
St Katherine's CP School, Snodland

Friends

F riends are pleasant
R apidly go around the park
I think they are brilliant
E nthral me at school
N oisy friends give me advice
D elight me up when I am sad
S neak behind my back and make me scared,
                         don't forget the word friends!

Wesley McCloud (11)
St Katherine's CP School, Snodland

Seasons

S un glistens and sparkles
U nder the sky so blue
M eant to make you feel shiny
M akes you go, *boo!*
E nds so quickly
R ain comes to you.

W inter makes you feel cool
I n the sky it's very grey
kN it your woolly jumper
T ry it on today
E ncourages you to stay warm
R ain goes and more seasons to come.

Rebecca Hawkes (10)
St Katherine's CP School, Snodland

Love

Love is pink like Lovehearts.
It tastes of sweets
It smells like fresh buttercups blooming
It looks like a rose on a summer's morning
It sounds like music to your ears
Love feels like cuddling a kitten for the first time
It is radiant in every way like a butterfly on a summer's day.

Jade Shepheard (8)
St Katherine's CP School, Snodland

Rain

Rain is really fun
Rain is really annoying
Rain falls on rooftops
Rain forms very big, grey clouds
Rain is very, very wet.

Daniel Simmons (9)
St Katherine's CP School, Snodland

Love

Love is as red as a heart.
Love tastes like pretty berries.
Love smells like juicy daisies.
Love looks like freshly cut grass.
Love sounds like birds chirping..
Love feels like butterflies fluttering.

Levi Bonage (8)
St Katherine's CP School, Snodland

Dolphins

D ancing dolphins drift away.
O il spills leak and sway.
L azy dolphins dip and dream, closer comes the oil cream
P assing through the cold wind
H elp is here to save the day.
I n and out the waves grow stronger
N ear the black dark grows longer and larger
S inging dolphins are here to play.

Coral Randall (11)
St Katherine's CP School, Snodland

Friends

F riends are fab
R eally cool
I think they're funny
E ven them all
N ot easy hard going
D elighted for them all
S o have a good day even at school.

Amy Vinten (10)
St Katherine's CP School, Snodland

Winter Rains

Rain, rain, rain
Why does it always?
It makes a lovely sound
And it trickles on the street
But all it does
Is fall a hundred feet
People might play around
But I don't think it's fun
Because rain just goes and comes
And soaks me to the sun
Cold, wet, penetrating winter rain
When will it be spring again?

Ellis West (9)
St Katherine's CP School, Snodland

The Clock

It rolls and rolls it never stops
Until the 4th of February comes and rocks
It swallows time and spits it out
It has one hand that ticks
And another that tocks
Time stands still momentarily
And then continues.

Liam Stocking (10)
St Katherine's CP School, Snodland

My Mum - Haiku

My mum might be big
My mum might be quite stressy
But she is my mum.

Paige Goodwin (10)
St Katherine's CP School, Snodland

Me And My Family

I'm sometimes good
But sometimes bad
Sometimes terrifying
Sometimes mad
I have a sister
And two brothers
If they're not nice
I make them pay a price
If they don't stop
I'll get fed up
So you better
Stop, stop, stop!

Tanya Sterrett (11)
St Katherine's CP School, Snodland

Friends

F riends are funny, friends are cool
R eally get on well
I really like them
E ven when they're annoying
N ever break up
D o always keep friends
S o have fun while you're young, keep your best friends.

Tom Crittenden (10)
St Katherine's CP School, Snodland

Love

The kissing lips, hugging arms, the holding hands,
Sparkly eyes, the minty breath, the box of chocolates
Wrapped-up presents, the sparkling dress
Golden jewels, the silver shoes and the red lipstick.
The white teeth, blonde hair and pink nail varnish
And a huge box of Cadbury's chocolate.

Sarah Kendall (11)
St Katherine's CP School, Snodland

Friday The 13th

On Friday the 13th my teacher fell over in a muddy puddle.
On Friday the 13th the door went into my friend's face.
On Friday the 13th the stapler went into my mummy's finger.
On Friday the 13th the paint went all over my daddy.
On Friday the 13th another teacher can't get in.
On Friday the 13th someone forgot their book bag.
On Friday the 13th someone fell over, then ten people fell over him
Friday the 13th.

Colleen Fitzpatrick (7)
St Paul's CE Primary School, Swanley Village

Money

There was a young man called Sonny,
He never ran out of money,
He works in a bank,
Keeps snakes in a tank,
And his snakes look after his money.

Alex Chapman (9)
St Paul's CE Primary School, Swanley Village

I See

I see I see a cat in a tree.
I see I see an itchy flea.
I see I see a buzzing bee.

I see I see
What do I see?
I know what I see
I see *me!*

Thomas Franklin (7)
St Paul's CE Primary School, Swanley Village

Ten Crazy Teachers

Ten crazy teachers standing in a line,
One went swimming and then there were nine.

Nine crazy teachers standing by a gate,
One went hang-gliding and then there were eight.

Eight crazy teachers standing up in Heaven,
One went to Devon and then there were seven.

Seven crazy teachers standing on some bricks,
One fell off and then there were six.

Six crazy teachers standing ready to dive,
One forgot her swimsuit and then there were five.

Five crazy teachers standing on the floor,
One did a cartwheel and then there were four.

Four crazy teachers climbing up a tree,
One joined the elephants and then there were three.

Three crazy teachers standing in the zoo,
One got sunburnt and then there was two.

One crazy teacher standing in the sun,
He got bored, went home and then there were none.

Jaymie-Leigh Horn (11)
St Paul's CE Primary School, Swanley Village

Wind - Haiku

The wind is so strong
It blows leaves onto the ground
It blows all around.

Daniel Ludlam (10)
St Paul's CE Primary School, Swanley Village

My Magic Box

(Based on 'Magic Box' by Kit Wright)

I will put inside my magic box
A camel fighting through the windy deserts.

I will put inside my magic box
A kangaroo boxing a tree.

I will put inside my magic box
An Egyptian pharaoh.

I will put inside my magic box
Footballers like Owen, Beckham and Heskey.

I will put inside my magic box
A boat with a BBQ floating over the blue sea.

My box glows through the night.

Dean Baldwin (10)
St Paul's CE Primary School, Swanley Village

My Magic Box

(Based on 'Magic Box' by Kit Wright)

I will put inside my magic box . . .
Happy times with all my friends and family,
One thousand secrets,
Memories of my best holidays.

I will put inside my magic box . . .
The miaow from a fluffy satisfied cat,
The wiggly ears from a sleepy rabbit,
And the glint from a glittery icicle.

My magic box has stars for hinges
And is lined with purple silk
And on the top is a light pink feather,
The rest of the sides are mirrors.
The look is made of smiles and the lid is a rainbow colour.

Laura Franklin (10)
St Paul's CE Primary School, Swanley Village

Chelsea

He made me an offer,
I just can't refuse,
A ticket to Chelsea,
To cheer on the blues.

So I took his ticket,
And got on the train,
We travelled to London,
To watch the game.

When we got there,
There was a huge crowd,
There was lots of noise
It was very, very loud.

When we sat down,
As the players came out,
I stood up and started
To shout.

When the game started,
I was cheering,
Then we scored,
And they started booing.

In the second half,
We scored three more,
But they made a come-back,
By scoring four.

It stayed as a draw,
But when time was nearly up,
We scored a goal,
And we won the cup!

Thomas Morey (9)
St Paul's CE Primary School, Swanley Village

My First Try

It was a freezing cold day
When we went off to play.
The tournament began
And everyone ran
The ball was in sight
And I grabbed with all my might
I had the ball under my arm
I had to keep calm
I ran to the end of the field
Without a gum shield
The ref's whistle blew
It was then that we knew
We had *won!*

Oliver Coe (9)
St Paul's CE Primary School, Swanley Village

The Naughty Kid

I once knew a kid,
His name was Sid,
You'll never guess what he did.

He blew up the school,
But looked like a fool,
Cos he really upset us all.

They took him away,
He had this to say,
'I wish I didn't do that today.'

Sonny Exeter (10)
St Paul's CE Primary School, Swanley Village

Ten Naughty Schoolboys

Ten naughty schoolboys walking in a line
One tripped over and then there were nine.

Nine naughty schoolboys got home late
One got told off and then there were eight.

Eight naughty schoolboys went to Devon
One drowned in the sea and then there were seven.

Seven naughty schoolboys playing with sticks
One got hit and then there were six.

Six naughty schoolboys saw a beehive
One was stung and then there were five.

Five naughty schoolboys played by a door
One hurt himself and then there were four.

Four naughty schoolboys had their tea
One was full up and then there were three.

Three naughty schoolboys went to the loo
One got locked in and then there were two.

Two naughty schoolboys did their homework
One was done and then there was one.

One naughty schoolboy stood all alone
He got upset so he went home.

Lucy Evans (9)
St Paul's CE Primary School, Swanley Village

The Storm - Haiku

Rough seas are crashing,
Wild stormy winds are blowing,
Darkness is spreading.

Gareth Clarridge (11)
St Paul's CE Primary School, Swanley Village

My Magic Box

(Based on 'Magic Box' by Kit Wright)

I will put in my magic box . . .

The memory of my birth
And I will put in my box a white tiger's tooth
And a sharp dinosaurs claw.

I will put in my magic box . . .

A feather from an eagle
And a flame from a dragon
And a blue magic feather.

I will put in my magic box . . .

My first season ticket to see Arsenal play
And I will put in my box a football kit.

My magic box will have sharp corners
And a star on the top with a blue lid and a blue bottom.

Daniel Humm (10)
St Paul's CE Primary School, Swanley Village

My Magic Box

(Based on 'Magic Box' by Kit Wright)

I will put inside my magic box . . .

A lifetime of chocolate bars,
I will put all my secrets for life.

I will put inside my magic box . . .
My memories of all my friends,
And my mum, dad and sister's happiness.

My magic box has stars on top,
Gold hinges and all my friends faces,
To remind me of them.

Chloe Webb (9)
St Paul's CE Primary School, Swanley Village

My Magic Box

(Based on 'Magic Box' by Kit Wright)

Inside my magic box . . .
I would keep,
A fox swimming in the sea.
I would put in a baton,
Flying through the air
Hitting the heads of enemies.
I would put in a new Busted CD.

Inside my magic box . . .
I would keep,
Memories from Hawaii,
Dancing in hula style,
I would put in beaches
From the Caribbean.

Inside my magic box . . .
I would keep,
My friends and family,
And my first date,
With Harry.

My box would be red velvet
With sparkling stars all over.
The hinges would be the shape of my heart
My box would be me.

Laura Townson (11)
St Paul's CE Primary School, Swanley Village

My Magic Box

(Based on 'Magic Box' by Kit Wright)

I will put inside my magic box . . .
The wonderful feeling of reaching the top of Snowdon,
All the secrets my diary knows,
All the laughs and tears with my friends,
My sequined tailcoat and sparkly shoes from the dance show.

I will put in my magic box . . .
The roar of a Tyrannosaurus,
The pad of a cheetah's feet,
The squeaking of the extinct dodo wishing the world farewell.

I will put in my magic box . . .
The sound of the sea in a shell,
The glitter of the sun on the water,
A pearl secretly forming in an oyster.

I will put in my magic box . . .
A life-size map of the world with every house marked,
A full scale model of the universe.

My magic box is made of a bubble,
With thought on the corners,
The lid made of a peacock feather,
The lock made out of stardust,
The key made out of every type of weather.

Hannah Waddington (10)
St Paul's CE Primary School, Swanley Village

My Little Brother George

My little brother George is cute and sweet.
To make him laugh you tickle his feet.
Most of the time he's full of joy,
But when he's not well he's a miserable little boy.

Harry Oborne (10)
St Paul's CE Primary School, Swanley Village

My Dream

My dream is counting sheep
Up and down the fields they go, jumping high and low.
Let's count the sheep, one, two, three, *whee!*
High up in the sky and over the fence.
Four, five, six as we pick up sticks.
Seven, eight, nine as we count them fine.
Ten, eleven, twelve.
Oh no, look at the time it's dinner, smells nice
Perhaps tomorrow maybe we can count again.

Alice Spinola (8)
St Paul's CE Primary School, Swanley Village

A Witch's Spell

Fin of shark and liver of lamb
Leg of toad and heart of man
Blood of cat and eye of newt
And a little bit of dog's puke.

Double, double, toil and trouble
Fire burn and cauldron bubble.

Toe of tiger and brain of rat
Gut of goat and head of bat
Finger of baby and lungs of snake
Ear of elephant and seaweed of lake.

Double, double, toil and trouble
Fire burn and cauldron bubble.

Jamie Buggy (8)
St Peter's CE Combined School, Slough

From A Railway Carriage

The train whistles and rumbles
Through meadows and stations
It vibrates and clatters
Past houses and bridges.

It hoots and it rattles
Through fields and cities
It puffs and it clambers
Past creatures and us
And here is a mill and there is a river
Each a glimpse and gone forever.

Charley Ringer (8)
St Peter's CE Combined School, Slough

From A Railway Carriage

The train choo, choos and woo, woos
Through stations and houses
It rumbles and rattles
Past bushes and bridges.

It puffs and it charges
Through fields and bushes
It smokes and it whistles
Past meadows and farms.

And here is a mill, and there is a river
Each a glimpse and gone forever!

Maverick Davies (8)
St Peter's CE Combined School, Slough

Yesterday Last Week

Yesterday last week
The world will walk on people
Food will eat children
And Mums will pick up toys.

Yesterday last week
Pigs will fly and birds will roll in mud
Shelves will go on children
And dictionaries will read children.

Yesterday last week
Pens will use children
You will say I'm a fairy
Yesterday last week.

Jovi Wilson (9)
St Peter's CE Combined School, Slough

Yesterday Next Week

Yesterday next week,
Marge will like doughnuts
Homer will be a househusband
Bart will play the saxophone
And Lisa will skate on the skateboard.

Yesterday next week
Bananas will eat monkeys
Shops will sell shopkeepers
Leopards will have stripes
And tigers will have spots.

Yesterday next week
Girls will be bald
Boys will be hairy
Forever.

Rumbi Mukundu (9)
St Peter's CE Combined School, Slough

From A Railway Carriage

The train rattles and battles
Through mountains and fountains
It rattles and clatters past bridges and fridges
It huffs and it whistles
Through trees and bees
It whizzes and it quizzes
Past battles and cattle.

Jamie Byne (9)
St Peter's CE Combined School, Slough

I Wish I Could Paint

I wish I could paint . . .
A sparkling star as bright as light
A speeding cheetah as fast as sight
A falling raindrop as blue as black
A field of flowers as far as a star.

Jonathan Pomry (9)
St Peter's CE Combined School, Slough

Wind

The wind blows north.
The wind blows forth.
The wind blows south.
It blows with its mouth.
The wind blows east.
It chatters my teeth
The wind blows west.
The wind blows the best.

Cameron Lovett (9)
St Peter's CE Combined School, Slough

Yesterday Next Week

Yesterday next week
Mums will do your homework
Dads will go to school and play bingo
And children will skip school and never go back.

Yesterday next week
Dogs will go bowling
Cats will kick a dog
And fish will sing the fish song.

Yesterday next week
Children will be the teachers
Teachers will be children
And parents will be rats
And nobody will tell me I've won the lotto.

Victoria Garnett (8)
St Peter's CE Combined School, Slough

Butterfly

I wish I could paint a butterfly.
As colourful as a rainbow.
As shiny as a diamond.
As beautiful as flower.
As small as a rubber.
As light as a feather,
As amazing as a unicorn,
As pretty as jewels,
And as rich as money.

Crystal Yang (9) & Jesskiran Kullar (8)
St Peter's CE Combined School, Slough

A Witch's Spell

Head of cat and eye of newt
And bit of child's puke.

Blood of lamb and liver of dog
And a bit of really ill hog.

Double, toil and trouble,
Fire burn and cauldron bubble.

Eye of cat and paw of lion
And a bit of Wilbur's blood.

Head of baby and eye of cat
And a big bit of some fat.

Double, double, toil and trouble
Fire burn and cauldron.

Lindsey Tanner
St Peter's CE Combined School, Slough

Goodnight Candlelight

There was a light
And it was so bright
Oh candlelight
You gave me a fright
I got cross
And told it off
So I squeezed it tight
And put out his light
Goodnight, goodnight,
Oh candlelight.

Kerri Thomas (9)
St Peter's CE Combined School, Slough

Winter Snow

Snow is white
It is bright and light
I think it's nice
Some people think it's sliced
It is wet
I caught it with a net
You can go swimming
But it is so shimmering
It is so cold
Some people think it's gold
I go to my room
And I see a spoon
I pick it up
And it turns into a cup.

Harry McGill (7)
St Teresa's Catholic Primary School, Wokingham

My Favourite Things

(Based on 'Pencil me In' by Benjamin Zephaniah)

I have a pencil full of red
I sleep with it in my bed
I even write on the garden shed
So that is why my pencil's red.

I have a friend that is full of fun
We had a race but she won
Her favourite food is hot cross bun
So that is why she's full of fun.

I have a toy full of hair
He looks a bit like the Mayor
He sits on my bedroom chair
So that is why he's full of hair.

Alice Graham (7)
St Teresa's Catholic Primary School, Wokingham

My Pencil

(Based on the poem 'Pencil Me In' by Benjamin Zephaniah)

I have a pencil full of red,
I sleep with it in my bed,
I write with one on the garden shed.

I have a pencil full of white,
It wakes me up in the middle of the night,
It gave me such a fright
That I had to turn on the light.

Megan Marks (7)
St Teresa's Catholic Primary School, Wokingham

Winter Snowflakes

Hear the snowflakes whirling down,
You can hear it everywhere in town,
It is shiny, white and shimmery
The snowflakes are very glimmering
It fades away as it touches the ground
The next one comes and floats around.

Imogen Stone (8)
St Teresa's Catholic Primary School, Wokingham

Snake

Snake crawling round a tree
Your skin is the colour of a pea.
Green and yellowy quite marshmallowy
Sliding along scale over scale
You blend with the tree, some dark some pale
Back to your den to sleep.

Lucy Farrell (7)
St Teresa's Catholic Primary School, Wokingham

Twister

I danced with cloud,
He twists me around as fast as a rollercoaster
I sucked up the earth
Like a hoover sucking up tiny bits of dirt
We went on all night
Until there was no light
We ate luscious green grass
We listened to the band, instruments all brass
I said 'Bye maybe we'll see each other another day'
We arranged to see each other next by the bay.

Anna Jones (8)
St Teresa's Catholic Primary School, Wokingham

Missing Card

I opened up a pack of cards
Only fifty-one!
Wonder where it could be hidden
It's spoiling all my fun!

Down the settee
No
Under the bed
No
On the TV
No
Over your head
No
Now Will he is my brother
He's quite a joker too
He had it all along
Now there's fifty-two!

Megan Shillibier (7)
St Teresa's Catholic Primary School, Wokingham

I Know A Little Brother

My little brother is very funny,
He likes playing with money.
I shout 'Stop being so rude.'
Then my brother gets in a bad mood.
My brother likes playing prince and princesses,
While my mum is writing addresses.
My brother loves Spider-Man,
He always sings 'Bob, the builder can he fix it?
Bob the builder, yes he can.'

Elliot Ball (8)
St Teresa's Catholic Primary School, Wokingham

Winter Weather

Soft as cotton
Never forgotten,
I pick it up
Shape it like a cup,
Nothing so white
I am right,
Nothing so shimmering
Or so glimmering.

Paige Blake (8)
St Teresa's Catholic Primary School, Wokingham

Winter Snow

Snow is amusing! Glorious!
Crunch, crunch as you walk through the snow.
White snow that covers the landscape.
Magnificent.
Falling, falling all the winter night,
Some people have a fright.
I like the snow because it's great
You feel like you want a date.

Joel Grist (8)
St Teresa's Catholic Primary School, Wokingham

You'd Better Believe Him

(Based on the poem 'You'd Better Believe Him' by Brian Patten)

Discovered an old teddy bear in Woolworths,
I asked her for her name but she didn't answer me,
So I took her home instead.
I called her little Alice but she didn't say a word.
So I took her for a walk and she acted like a worm.
I took her back home and she asked me for my name
So I said I was Anna and she never asked again.

Amy James (7)
St Teresa's Catholic Primary School, Wokingham

You'd Better Believe Her

(Based on the poem 'You'd Better Believe him' by Brian Patten)

Discovered a new teddy bear in Woolworths,
She tried to cuddle it but without much luck.
It had a red bow,
And it sat in a row.
She went to the till,
But she didn't get her bill.
She said 'Can I buy him please?'
I pleased, but she just teased.

Gemma Boucher (7)
St Teresa's Catholic Primary School, Wokingham

Snow

I sprinkled down like snow
Really, really low
I landed on the ground
And made a little sound
I felt like I was wet
And I was very nearly set
To have some fun
But not in the sun.

Catherine Barnes (9)
St Teresa's Catholic Primary School, Wokingham

The Sun

I baked the town and boiled the people,
I never go down,
People think it's scorching hot,
Others think it's freezing cold.

People think it's a terrible disaster,
I sob and say 'Well tough luck you're in the way
You people will bear with it some day.'

Moaning people that's what's making me sad
I think I should leave the town after all,
They'll feel better with only the moon,
I'm leaving so boo hoo.

People now wake up when the alarm clock rings,
They say 'Where is the sun?'
The people moan without me,
I think I shall come back again.
Now people don't moan again.

Antiana Loxha (8)
St Teresa's Catholic Primary School, Wokingham

Twister

I hope he will never come again that nasty monster Twister.
You said that you will never come again but you did.
You lied to me you nasty twister.
You twisted me around, up, down
And you hurt the turtles and the bunnies.
I hope he will never come again that nasty Mister Twister.
You ate us out of the house and all the children you hurt us,
You hurt us, you nasty Mister Twister.
You took all our friends and family.
We don't like you Mister Twister.
I hope he will never come again that nasty Mister Twister
And he did!

Thomas Mitchell (9)
St Teresa's Catholic Primary School, Wokingham

Sunny Weather

In the south at the beach
Tons of people rushing in and out.
The sun pushes the wind away
And the clouds stay away to the north.
I could hear the sea whistling like a human
The fish floated around in the cooling sea.

Jack Murray (8)
St Teresa's Catholic Primary School, Wokingham

Sloth

I have a sloth in me,
Moving, slowly,
Dozing, sleepily,
Scrunching leaves,
Swimming speedily,
Everyone looking for me.
Everyone caring as they look.
I must get away.

Joseph Crolla (8)
St Teresa's Catholic Primary School, Wokingham

Hot Weather

A knuckle of sun,
A nice hot cross bun.
The hot sun like an oven,
People sunbathing, loving it
Until the big sun came out.
The lush green grass wilting
The wind swaying
Everything is lush
I am going to sleep
Now hush.

Gabby Pitts (8)
St Teresa's Catholic Primary School, Wokingham

Bad Weather

That hurricane is bad weather
Now the chicken has one feather.

He was smashing the fences and thrashing the houses
He even scared all the mouses.

That hurricane is bad weather
Now the chicken has one feather.

No more dogs
No more water hogs
No more cats
No more rats
There's no more noise
There are no toys
Just a silent gentle breeze.

Jack Hughes (9)
St Teresa's Catholic Primary School, Wokingham

Snow Fairy

Snow in morning,
Snow in night,
You can see little sparkles come from the sky.
Here and there and everywhere,
Watch the snowflakes swirling down,
Making snowmen in the snow.
Baking warm, toasty cookies.
Time for bed snuggling up under the covers,
Next morning 'No snow' I cry
But I hope snow comes another day!

Sophie Hastings (8)
St Teresa's Catholic Primary School, Wokingham

Clouds

Wind, wind, wonderful wind and colourful
Clouds!
A breeze flutters by,
Like a butterfly,
And then,
All of a sudden,
A shadow rears,
And the sheep were at the shears,
The sheep are going to be sheared,
By the farmer.

Wind, wind, wonderful wind and colourful
Clouds!

A drizzle quacks and flies,
Across the rain drown skies,
And then,
All of a sudden,
The sun hops out. *Ouch!*
The rays pop out of the pouch.
The clouds come up,
And the dog hurdles them away
Sun, sun, clouds, clouds
Wonderful!

Eloise Utley (8)
St Teresa's Catholic Primary School, Wokingham

Hedgehog

I have a hedgehog in me,
Slyly hiding,
Sniffing loudly,
Moving sneakily,
Running fast,
Rustling in the leaves,
Nobody cares for me,
Nobody needs me,
 I am alone.

Alicia Clark (9)
St Teresa's Catholic Primary School, Wokingham

Blizzard

Twirling snowflakes come drifting down
Into the frozen town
Snowflakes bang on the windowpane
It looks a bit like heavy rain
The power's gone off there is no light
Now even the ghosts are in fright
When that blizzard hit the town
It sent everyone's dogs round and round
I hope I'll never see that blizzard again.

Alice Wilson (8)
St Teresa's Catholic Primary School, Wokingham

Sun

The sun
Is always fun
Its light is always bright
But the snow is always white
The sun looks like gold
The font big and bold
So please sun
Please come again.

Lauren Olivia Booth (8)
St Teresa's Catholic Primary School, Wokingham

Snow Queen

I put some ice on the land,
And made some snow out of sand.
I made a snowflake out of snow,
The best I have ever known.
I made all the trees gleaming bright,
My little white dove made some light.
The sun comes up and it fears,
That I have come and disappeared.

Hannah Lyle (8)
St Teresa's Catholic Primary School, Wokingham

Storm

I have a temper,
That's right to be,
For I can cackle and boom
To kingdom come,
They fear for me.

I scowl at the people below,
I will thrash you if you get in my way.
I punch and crunch
To volley the road
They fear for me.

I send trees flying,
I tear apart houses,
I ruin the towns,
They fear for me.

I claw the city sharply
They fear for me.

I am the most aggressive in the world.

Bethan Davies (8)
St Teresa's Catholic Primary School, Wokingham

Snow Fairy

Sparkling, shimmering
No glistening, gleaming
Oh how I love snow
Wow, lovely snow clean and white.

Fabulous fairy
Attractive too
Innocent arrivals
Ruby red, best in bed
Yellow gold.

Hannah Poland (8)
St Teresa's Catholic Primary School, Wokingham

Snowflake

I brushed snow off my window ledge,
Then went outside and played on my sledge.

I heard the church bells ding
Then my heart began to sing.

I couldn't believe it was Christmas Day
I ran to my friends and went to play.

The gleaming white snow was so crunchy
The lovely roast turkey was munchy.

Christmas is such fun
But I can't wait for the sun!

Sasha Gama (8)
St Teresa's Catholic Primary School, Wokingham

The Great White Shark

I've got a pet great white shark,
I keep him at the park,
He eats small fish,
He ate my mum's best dish.
He is grey and white,
He gives other people a right old fright!
Once I kept him in a bath,
But my mum said 'Drag him up the garden path'
He can play ball games,
And plays pool games
My pet great white shark can be a right old laugh.

Sarah Rafferty (9)
St Teresa's Catholic Primary School, Wokingham

I Am A Tornado

I am a tornado,
And I am Mr Destroyer.

I am speeding round,
I am destroying the world,
I am petrifying little children and families,
I am making people fly.

I am a tornado
And I am Mr Destroyer.

I am speeding round
I am destroying the world.
I am knocking down houses and buildings
I am *deadly*.
I am a tornado
And I am coming for
You!

Matthew Sanderson (8)
St Teresa's Catholic Primary School, Wokingham

Snow Fall

I sprinkle gently on the ground
I don't make a sound
I cover all around.

When I float at night
I fly like a kite
Giving painful frostbite.

I will melt when the sun's on track,
Goodbye my friends, I will come back
See you soon, my good friend Jack.

Nicola Relf (8)
St Teresa's Catholic Primary School, Wokingham

The Storm

Wind and rain
Don't come again.

You thrash
And bash
You gloom
And doom
My town today
So go away.

Wind and rain
Don't come again.

Go away leave us all
You're not hot and you're not cool
When I want to go out you're still here
Just go away for another year.

Wind and rain
Don't come again.

You're as busy as a bee
You knock down trees,
Please don't stay
Go away!

Wind and rain
Don't come again.

Hey! You've stopped
Going plip plop.

Judith Taylor (9)
St Teresa's Catholic Primary School, Wokingham

I Am The Snow

I am the snow
That comes and goes
As cold as ice
Sometimes as little as mice.

I am the snow
That comes and goes
As soft as
Cotton wool.

I am the snow
That comes and goes
As white as
White chocolate.

I am the snow
That comes and goes
That gets thrown around
And played with.

I am the snow
That comes and goes
I am loved by children
All over the world.

Aaron Morjaria (9)
St Teresa's Catholic Primary School, Wokingham

I See A Dog

I see a dog
That is chasing a ball
Carelessly into a wall
It is as black as night
With a red nose where he hurt himself
Funky fat Labrador
Soft, smooth fluffy fur
A loud howling bark.

Matthew Dodington (8)
St Teresa's Catholic Primary School, Wokingham

Rain

Rain
You are a pain
So please don't come again.

Don't thrash down on the ground
Don't swirl yourself around.

Rain
You are a pain
So please don't come again.

Don't make the ground wet
Don't wait for it to set.

Rain
You are a pain
So please don't come again.

Please don't stay
Please go away.

Meg Martin (9)
St Teresa's Catholic Primary School, Wokingham

I See A Dog

I see a dog
Bouncing around happily in the field
Jumps quickly
Smoothing white
Long thin body
White smooth fur
Barks at everybody coming in
It runs straight at the wall
That's my dog Gemma.

Olivia Reilly (8)
St Teresa's Catholic Primary School, Wokingham

My Bedroom

Inside my bedroom
It's like the hot beach,
With the sound
Of the calm waves,
Coming onto the soft sand.
The rocks are grey
And shiny.
The kids are throwing sand
All about,
Then a van comes up and there's
Ice cream!
Inside my bedroom
It's like a rabbit's burrow,
All dusty and musty.
It's as dirty as
A baby covered
In brown,
Sloppy,
Mud
And for a bed it's just leaves
And grass
With mud holding it together.
It's like a
Deep
Dark, brown
Tunnel
It's like a
Foxes
Den as well!

Kirstie McFarlane (8)
Seabrook CE Controlled Primary School, Hythe

Haikus For Valentines Day!

I waited for you
In the Hong Kong restaurant
But you did not come.

I waited for you
In the wild African bush
But you did not come.

I waited for you
On Valentines Day and yes
This time you did come.

I froze with delight
But you left without sorrow
And left me behind.

Jason Jordaan (8)
Seabrook CE Controlled Primary School, Hythe

Sea - Haiku

The sea is wavy
Like the wind in the sky, blue
It pushes you down.

The sea is quite rough
The sea leads you to the sun
You can't see a thing.

The sea is stormy
The children play in the sea
I see a rainbow.

Reece Bishop (9)
Seabrook CE Controlled Primary School, Hythe

In The Wood - Haiku

In the shady wood
There are huge squelchy puddles
The trees are so tall.

There is a car tyre
Where you can swing really high
The tyre is black.

If you climb the tree
You think you are in the sky
The tree is so high.

Isobel Lamb (8)
Seabrook CE Controlled Primary School, Hythe

The Sea

As I stumble in and out,
I sneak towards your toes,
I feel as I'm as calm as a smooth stone,
I am as lonely as a lost snail.

As I wait for my next victim,
I shiver with laughter,
I splash myself up against the rocks.
My heart sinks deep inside me,
And I feel as though I have no friends beside me.

Paul Croucher (10)
Seabrook CE Controlled Primary School, Hythe

War

I see death and destruction,
Gutted bodies and women and children screaming.
Burning buildings, burning bodies they all seem the same to me,
Except one has a soul, but the soul of war is the machine of war and
It will drive on to destroy lives and take souls to make mine stronger.
I feel joy and happiness as I bathe in blood from lost men,
I feel I can strengthen my reach into taking more lives,
I steal through the air seeing miserable men,
Crying for their lost friends,
Then I feel guilt,
I stop to think amongst the explosions and screaming,
Was this the right thing to do?
Shouldn't I have let my brother's diplomacy sort this out?
But then I remember I feel nothing. I smell sour blood,
Foul hatred shared between the two sides,
Bullets whiz and flicker past men.
I smell the fear in men as they charge into battle facing the
                                bombs and war,
My war.
Then, everything is quiet,
Everyone dead,
I faint away, until the next time,
Diplomacy fails.

Tomas Lamb (10)
Seabrook CE Controlled Primary School, Hythe

The Desert

The desert is hot
At night it is very cold
I couldn't stay there
Help me, somebody help me,
Somebody came to help me.

Nicole Baines (9)
Seabrook CE Controlled Primary School, Hythe

War

I am the one who creates the misery.
Do I care? I do not now.
All the weeping, all the heart breaking makes me laugh hysterically.
I am your worst nightmare.
I see through all your doom and darkness,
Shadows collapsing to the dusty ground,
As if I was a white sheet, all your rose-red bloodstains on me.

I smell the choking smoke and all of the dead bodies rotting away.
Oh I love the fun I am having.
All the distress, the pain and agony.
You thought I had gone; well, now I'm back,
I'm in action so beware my friends.
One strike of my power and an explosion is done,
The fire spits like a poisonous snake and
I hear the screams and shouts again;
It brings a shiver down my spine.
I'm like a god I suppose . . .

But what is this? The mist is disappearing, soldiers are going home,
There on the battlefield is a poppy which has bloomed.
Oh no my enemy has come, peace is in the land,
So the plug has been pulled, I'm locked back up in my cage;
But I may be lurking around the corner.

Alethia Hoad (9)
Seabrook CE Controlled Primary School, Hythe

The King

The king, predator
A real stunner,
Fast runner
Ferocious killer.

Kimberley Whitehead (10)
Seabrook CE Controlled Primary School, Hythe

War

I see dead bodies, as loved ones would say family.
I see tears and agony on peoples faces.
I look out and see people praying.
I see flames of things and which is now ash.
I see your worst nightmare but I'm still joyful.

I feel my heart throbbing,
It's going to explode from all the excitement.
I feel myself being destroyed.
I feel the soldier's feelings.
I feel the bullet go through me.
I feel I am in the war but I'm not.

I hear moaning from those who are dying.
I hear guns as the bullets go whizzing past.
I hear bombs as they explode on the ground.
I hear the sound of distress and laugh
I hear the sound of my thoughts, good thoughts my war.

I think great things of war.
I think war is for devils.
I think war is great.
I think war is a nightmare for everyone but me.

Katie Horne (10)
Seabrook CE Controlled Primary School, Hythe

Ghost!

I know a ghost,
He floats around,
A haunted house,
Not making a sound!

It lives inside,
This haunted house,
Coming out at midnight,
Only to see a mouse!

Amy Howarth (11)
Seabrook CE Controlled Primary School, Hythe

Witch's Brew

Double, double toil and trouble,
Fire burn and cauldron bubble,
Toad's liver,
Goo of river,
Blood of dog,
Leg of frog.

Double, double, toil and trouble,
Fire burn and cauldron bubble,
Claw of cat,
Eye of rat,
Wing of bat,
Chunk of fat.

Double, double, toil and trouble
Fire burn and cauldron bubble,
Wool of rotting sheep,
Leg of corroding meat,
Tail of newt
Rotting fruit.

James Whybrow (9)
Seabrook CE Controlled Primary School, Hythe

The Life Of A Smart Board

My job is to bother people
Beware
I like to tease you
Beware
I hate people poking me, pushing and patting me
Beware
I like annoying people especially teachers
So beware, teachers!

Harriet Drury (10)
Seabrook CE Controlled Primary School, Hythe

War

I see fear everywhere, sadness too,
I see hatred and carnage.
I see faces torn to nothing,
I feel fine!

I feel joyous,
I feel no regret.
I feel agony it relieves me from this happiness.

I feel pain.
I feel merciless,
I feel fine!

I think of happiness, it tears me apart,
I think of when this is over, when I am no more.
I think of death and devastation and it lifts me up,
I think of when joy is just a dream and it fills me with life,
I feel fine!

I smell death in the air.

I smell carcasses lying on the ground.
I smell people wounded,
I smell people dying, drawing in the last breath,
I feel fine!

I hear people crying out for life,
I hear yells of pain.
I hear bombs dropping
I hear bullets being fired.
I feel fine!

Lauren Connolly (11)
Seabrook CE Controlled Primary School, Hythe

War

I stand watching all of those people
Wanting their loved ones to be near to them.
Dying in agony, bleeding to death, tears dropping from people's eyes
Wondering if anyone's coming to help them.
Flames from bombs gradually getting higher.
People running from fear,
I feel joyful inside for what I have done,
I feel laughter in my stomach.
I feel inside me what people don't feel inside themselves.
I feel evil but I still feel very strong.
I think of the things that I have done.
I think of what I have done to my world
But I am still very happy, happy, happy.
I smell the black smoke that's in the cloudy sky.
I smell red blood everywhere from bullets in people's bodies.
I smell carnage, but still feel happy.
I hear people crying and calling for help but I still smile.
Everything I hear and everything I see
Still makes me have a smile on my face and it
I still laugh, laugh and laugh!

Rhea Giles (9)
Seabrook CE Controlled Primary School, Hythe